The Secr‹

MW01273571

"Christopher Foster's collection of quotations and reflective essays is full of generous insight and truth-telling. Its graceful companionship will be welcomed by readers of every age."
– Sharon Salzberg, author,
Real Happiness and Lovingkindness

"This is a bright and insightful book, and actually useful for any age! Naturally, it's also focused on aging, and can ease that glide path considerably."
– Ken Wilber, author, The Integral Vision

"Given that our flight from the process of aging and mortality is the chief neurosis of our time, Christopher Foster's reflections are most welcome for they summon the reader to thoughtful reflection, to the courage of convictions, and to a more considered embrace of the wonder, terror, and gift of this brief journey we call our lives."
– James Hollis, Ph.D., author, What Matters Most

"Are you aging? Then run, don't walk, to get this lovely book. Now in his 80's, Christopher Foster tells it like it is and so beautifully offers insights and practical suggestions to soften and sweeten the journey. This book is a rare blend of clarity and heart.

The Secret Promise of Aging

Miners Bay Books
Fernhill Centre
Mayne Island, BC

Apply its timeless lessons, and you, like Christopher, will dwell in peace and fulfillment regardless of your age."
    – Gail Brenner, Ph.D., psychologist and blogger, AFlourishingLife.com

"This is one of the most inspiring books to come my way. Christopher Foster is a beacon for all those who want to live a fulfilling and fruitful life – especially at a mature age. This book will not only make your day, it will make your year."
    – Mary Jaksch, blogger, GoodLifeZen.com, co-founder, The A-List Blogger Club

"Christopher Foster's The Secret Promise of Aging is a most uplifting book and 'must read' for all ages. He is an inspiration and his life and books are a testament to the fact that our spirit remains ever ageless."
    – Angela Artemis, author, The Intuition Principle

"Christopher's story on its own is awe-inspiring. His message about aging is revolutionary. He is right; age need not be a barrier or a restriction. Older people often feel redundant and yet they are really wonderful, exciting human beings with all this wisdom and experience to share. That said, the book deals with so much more than aging and each chapter shares the author's profound and also touching wisdom."
    – Kim Masters, blogger, Dream-OnBlog.com

"This is an amazing and thought-provoking book on how to live in the moment and expand your joy. This isn't a book you should rush through, but one you should read a few pages, contemplate, and apply to your life immediately. Highly recommended for anyone who has difficulty finding joy in their day-to-day life, as well as those who need inspiration and comfort."
– Marilyn Doren, student, Applied Equine Podiatry

"Every once in a while an author and a book appear which inspire and transform our understanding of ourselves at a heart and soul level. Christopher Foster is a wise expert in making others feel good about aging with joy and grace. The Secret Promise of Aging is a must read for anyone who looks in the mirror and dreads what they see!"
– Tess Marshall, blogger, TheBoldLife.com

"The Secret Promise of Aging is for you. Be you young or old, you will find this to be a spirited and spiritual adventure book. This man has lived. And he doesn't pull punches. Within the first few chapters Christopher confronts head on some lacerating life events most of us hope to bypass. This is no elevator music, this is Zen jazz. Taut, potent and compelling."
– Evan Griffith, blogger, TheWorldIsFreakyBeautiful.com

"The Secret Promise of Aging is a unique gift to us all, no matter what our age. His writings soothe and assure that we are loved just as we are."
        –Maureen Moeller, Counselor, M.S. Ed

"I definitely recommend this book to anybody, old or young. Younger ones would benefit from Christopher's viewpoints about LIFE that if accepted and implemented will bring a well-rounded and happier life."
        – Kenneth L. Lim, Doctor of Chiropractic

"This book will appeal to many ages. It addresses many circumstances and contains many stories that I am positive will resonate in many lives. It is the type of book that will be read, re-read, and read again. Humanity knows many languages and Foster has the gift of speaking them all."
        – Risa McFarland, Montessori M.T., Community
                Child Advocate

"In the midst of our busy lives, it is great to be reminded of that refuge of peacefulness that Foster calls 'true nature.' My father's book is full of such pointers to the truth of ourselves, and thus I highly recommend it."
        – Durwin Foster, M.A.

The Secret Promise of Aging

Finding Meaning, Joy and Inner Peace as Years Fly By

Christopher Foster

Special thanks to Maddi Newman of Keyboard
Graphic Design, Martha Bullen of Bullen
Publishing Services, and Carol Leavenworth,
Jungian therapist.

Published by Singing Spirit Books
Centennial, Colorado 80122 USA

ISBN – 13: 978-0-9711796-2-2

Book design and layout by:
KeyBoard Graphic Design, Print and Web
www.maddi.ca

For my wife, JoAnn and my son, Durwin.

Also by Christopher Foster:

Fiction:

The Raven Who Spoke with God

Winds Across the Sky

Bearers of the Sun

Biography:

One Heart, One Way

Poetry collections:

A Time for Heroes

The Transcendent Nation

Contents

Introduction

Part One: Meaning

Part Two: Joy

Part Three: Inner Peace

Afterword

Introduction

It's Never Too Late
to Live Your Dream

"It is never too late to turn on the light. Your ability to break an unhealthy habit or turn off an old tape doesn't depend on how long it has been running; a shift in perspective doesn't depend on how long you've held on to the old view. When you flip the switch in that attic, it doesn't matter whether it's been dark for ten minutes, ten years or ten decades."
— Sharon Salzberg

"As you move toward a dream, the dream moves toward you."
— Julia Cameron

I love the truth articulated in Sharon Salzberg's quote. It's never too late to "turn on the light." It's never too late to change. And most importantly, it's never too late to live your dream and create a new future for yourself.

As long as you are here, as long as you are still breathing, it doesn't really matter what your age is. The dream that you brought with you when you came into the world is calling to you still, wanting to be born in new and imaginative ways.

The dream that has animated me for as long as I can remember is to do whatever I can to give courage, comfort and peace to others through writing. But oh dear. Oh my gosh. The calendar says I'm in my 80s. Maybe it's time to call it quits and let go of my dream – to live my remaining days in peace and quiet, perhaps with a little touch of apathy thrown in?

I don't think so. "Not on your life," I hear my spirit say.

"You're just getting started. I've gone to a lot of trouble helping you through difficult times and inspiring you to keep growing. You're just beginning to get the hang of how life works and what you have learned can be helpful to others, so listen up.

"This is no time to think about 'retirement.' This is a time to stretch your wings like never before and fulfill your mission. You have an opportunity to create a new future for yourself that will be a blessing to others, so hop to it."

The general consensus in our culture seems to be that the older we grow the less useful and relevant we become. And if you haven't manifested your dream by age 40 or 50 or 60 or whatever, well, that's just too bad, you probably never will manifest it now.

I say that is false. Aging is a privilege. The older we are, the more opportunity we've had to learn life's ways and the more wisdom and compassion we have available to share with our world.

It's never too late to give your gift. It's never too late to create your preferred future. It's never too late to fulfill your dream. You know so much. You have proved so much. You have suffered so much and overcome so much. You have shed so many illusions and pretenses.

You are more authentic now than at any time in your life.

The world yearns for the light that is yours to share. It is the light of your own eternal spirit and it will never dim. I hope you enjoy my essays and I wish you good luck and God speed.

Part One

Meaning

Chapter 1

Fulfilling Our Destiny as We Age

*"We are born with a great dream for our lives — a
dream which may have been derailed along the way
by family and career or submerged by our own
choices. In the second half of life, it is time to resurrect
this dream."*

— Angeles Arrien

*"Most of us lead far more meaningful lives than we
know. Often finding meaning is not about doing things
differently; it is about seeing familiar things in new
ways."*

— Rachel Naomi Remen

A blizzard has dumped a pile of snow on Denver
overnight. The snow is at least a foot deep,
perhaps more. I peer out the window upon arising
and see a remarkable sight. Maxwell, a neighbor's
child, three years old and a good buddy of mine, is
already hard at work.

Safely bundled up in a thick, warm parka, the
intrepid young explorer struggles through the deep

snow, tugging a snow shovel behind him that is bigger than he is. Only about half of him shows above the snow, but what does he care? Maxwell loves doing manual work like grown-ups do.

When the garbage truck arrives on its weekly visit to our neighborhood, for example, who is outside to watch and supervise? Maxwell. He wouldn't miss this event for anything. He is never happier than when he is cutting grass with his toy lawn-mower – or helping the men lay new water-pipes – or, as is the case right now, when he can help clear some snow.

I watch, enchanted, as he selects a suitable spot, lifts his shovel, and attacks the snow covering the path that winds through our townhome complex. And I realize, as I savor the magic of the moment, that though my body is aging, I love life more deeply than ever. I am happier than I have ever been. I experience an increasing sense of oneness with creation and a deepening appreciation for its beauty and its many gifts to us.

Aging does not need to be a journey into decline. Not every moment of my life is beautiful or trouble-free, of course. But as I move along in my 80s I realize more clearly every day that aging is rightly a journey of discovery boundless in its possibilities and potential.

Obviously, growing older does bring challenges of many kinds. But challenges, as so many people have discovered, can be a catalyst that helps us change, and grow, and become more authentic and whole.

I experienced challenging times in 2005. At the age of 74 – following a series of dire events in my life – I found myself in the grip of a major clinical depression.

It was a horrific experience that lasted a full year, robbing me of energy and stripping the flesh from my bones. I'm a thin guy anyway, but watched helpless as my weight plummeted from 150 to 128 pounds. I despaired for my life. Even my wife, JoAnn, a stout-hearted soul who cared for me with unflinching courage, doubted at times if I would heal and dreaded what each new day might bring.

I was virtually housebound for months. How can I forget the sight of JoAnn working patiently every day at a difficult jigsaw puzzle to help her stay focused and forget her worries. How can I forget the moment when she came to me as I sat mute, bowed with grief at the kitchen table, and put her arms around me. She was quiet for a little while. Then she said simply, "I love you." I would not have survived without her care and love.

We tried everything, including therapy, medication, naturopathy, and a week at a behavioral health hospital in Denver, but nothing seemed to help. A local naturopath, a good friend, stopped calling me at a certain point – as he told me later – because he was afraid of what he might hear, and because he was convinced there was nothing more he could do.

But then – and this is the good part – a miracle. A moment of grace I shall never forget.

I had walked to the corner on slightly unsteady legs to pick up our mail when I experienced a moment of stillness, pure, fathomless, and unexpected, that set me free.

I felt a sense of freedom that is hard to define. I realized, in that moment of transformation, that the real "me" was untouched by my troubles. In fact, it was untouched by any of the misfortunes of my life, just as it was untouched by any of my past successes or achievements.

I realized too, in that magical moment, that the stillness I was experiencing didn't come from somewhere else, a separate, faraway deity perhaps. No. It was my own stillness. It was the stillness of being that abides in each one of us and invites all of us home in these troubled times.

You are not the helpless creature you may have been told you are. The dream of greatness you brought with you into the world is alive and well still and yearns to express itself through you more fully regardless of your age or circumstances.

We are spiritual beings with a unique gift to give and a unique destiny to fulfill. We don't have to become angry or embittered as we age. We can heed the words of Maggie Kuhn, founder of the

Gray Panthers, who famously declared, "We must always be open to each new day, to the future, to new opportunities. They're there, but we have to be ready to see them."

We are creators, and if we wish to enjoy meaning and happiness as we age, we must be alert to any opportunity to nurture the creative fire that is in us.

There are countless ways to express your love and stay relevant and engaged. For example, my wife, JoAnn loves quilting. She throws heart and soul into it. "A quilt is a blanket of love," she likes to say. For myself, besides walking and going to the coffee shop and working out at the gym and watching birds – and listening to the sounds of a nearby creek – I love blogging. I heartily recommend blogging to anyone of mature years looking for a new and rewarding activity.

It costs little, if anything, to start a blog. It has its challenges, of course. And it can be quite addictive. But I find it is a remarkable way to keep my mind sharp and stay connected with the rest of our struggling race. Having to think, each week, how I can offer something useful or meaningful in my posts helps give a focus for my life. And the feedback I receive from readers is sometimes so touching I am close to tears.

What's the greatest benefit of aging? For me, it is this. Aging gives us opportunity, if we are so blessed, to change and let ourselves grow and expand in new ways. There is a beautiful quote in Psalm 92:14 that should be plastered on every billboard in the country. "Still bearing fruit in old age, still remaining fresh and green."

That's you. That's me. That's each of us as we trust life and listen to the sweet, strong voice of our own heart.

Chapter 2

How Freddy the Fox
Helped Me Heal

*"Until one has loved an animal, a part of one's soul
remains unawakened."*
                                                 – Anatole France

*"If a culture treats a particular illness with
compassion and enlightened understanding, then
sickness can be seen as a challenge, as a healing
crisis and opportunity. When sickness is viewed
positively, then illness has a much better chance to
heal, with the concomitant result that the entire
person may grow and be enriched in the process."*
                                                 – Ken Wilber

I love Ken Wilber's words.

A few years ago, as I mentioned in the previous
chapter, a major depression – or was it a spiritual
crisis? – swept into my life like a tsunami one
evening.

In the midst of this dark period, probably the
biggest challenge I have ever faced, an interesting

event occurred. I looked out our living room window on a beautiful late summer day and saw a young fox walk casually across our front lawn.

The fox passed only about ten feet away from the window where I was watching.

Goodness, he was gorgeous. He was utterly at ease and at peace with life – though it seemed to me he was taking some chances ambling around a fairly busy subdivision like this – and a long, elegant tail streamed behind him like a flag blowing in the wind.

Suddenly Freddy, as I called him, decided a rest was in order. He stretched out deliciously on his belly beside our weeping cherry tree, pushing his rear legs out flat behind him as far as they would go, and then, with a grin of pure satisfaction, he slowly and deliberately lowered his chin onto his front paws and closed his eyes.

When I looked out later in the day, Freddy was gone. I thought I would never see him again. But I was wrong.

The young fox stayed with us for three weeks, sleeping beneath a lilac bush in our backyard, perfectly at home in a growing city of more than 50,000 people, surrounded by pick-ups and cars, children and dogs. He exemplified trust in every moment – whether curling up contentedly under the lilac bush for a snooze, or walking casually and effortlessly along the top of the wooden fence in our backyard, calmly ignoring the agitated yaps of a neighbor's dogs.

Perhaps it was mere chance Freddy came to visit when he did. But I like to think he was sent by a loving universe to keep me company and give me solace and hope during my ordeal.

Why do I think this? Because soon after he came to visit I began to get better. I emerged from the whole terrifying experience stronger and healthier than before I got sick.

It was not only a young fox who came to visit during this difficult time in my life. A robin – whom we named Ruby – chose to build her nest in a bush near our front door, and helped to lift our spirits also. We worried she might be frightened away when the postman or other people came to the door, but she stayed put. What a pleasure and deep, gut joy it was to peer silently into the bush once in a while and see the tip of her beak jutting out over the nest.

One day we didn't see Freddy any more. One day we didn't see Ruby any more either. And one day I threw away the medication a Kaiser psychiatrist had given me – which never really worked anyway – and began working out at a local gym. An angel named Robin, a trainer with a soft spot for seniors, took me under her wing and helped me regain lost muscle and energy.

I discovered how to smile and how to laugh again. It's pretty tough not being able to laugh for a whole year. I began to be at ease again in public. The natural lightness and joy of being began to flow through me once again. As Ken Wilber suggests in his quote, I began to realize that my illness was actually a door to a new life.

I'd like to share these beautiful words from Wendell Berry:

"When despair for the world grows in me
and I wake in the night at the least sound
in fear of what my life and my children's lives may be,
I go and lie down where the wood drake
rests in his beauty on the water, and the great heron
feeds."

Chapter 3

Why Should Young People Have All the Fun?

"What we all want is to continually grow and expand. I've discovered that as the body becomes more limited, the soul expands. And there is a full circle. A 2-year-old will pick up a leaf and look at it with fascination. You get to the other end and again are looking at a leaf. I know I am."
– Dustin Hoffman (from an interview in AARP Magazine)

"But if we are truly happy inside, then age brings with it a maturity, a depth, and a power that only magnifies our radiance."
– David Deida

Why should young people have all the fun? "Don't die before you die," are words worth remembering.

Consider the remarkable story of Anthony Smith. He's an Englishman who not so long ago, at the age of 85, fulfilled a boyhood dream when he crossed the Atlantic on a raft with three friends.

Crazy, right? Quite insane. Many people might think he needs to act his age. But oh my, what an adventure. It took about two months, according to reports, and was a reasonably smooth crossing except that the sail-driven raft suffered damage to two of its rudders.

Arriving in the Caribbean island of St. Maarten, Smith told a reporter from The Associated Press, "Some people say it was mad. But it wasn't mad. What else do you do when you get on in years?"

The purpose of the voyage, the crew explained, was to raise awareness about the environment, and also to prove that the elderly can do remarkable things. Things that some might consider dangerous. Things that they themselves – or other people – might have thought were beyond them.

Incidentally, the project was also designed to raise money for a British nonprofit called WaterAid, which makes potable water available to poor communities.

It was a bit of bad luck, curiously, that paid for the trip. Smith was injured when he was hit by a van. "I got some compensation," he told reporters. "So what do you blow the compensation money on? You blow it on a raft."

A different kind of challenge – calling for exactly the same kind of courage and presence of mind – faced Helen Collins when her husband, 81, suffered a fatal heart attack while piloting their light plane over Wisconsin.

The couple was flying back to Wisconsin from a weekend visit to Florida. As reported by NBC News, Helen had little experience flying planes, but was forced to take the controls and make an emergency landing on her own.

She stayed calm, and called the sheriff's dispatch center for help, her son, Richard, told MSNBC.com. "She was circling for an hour-and-a-half when the tanks were actually registering no fuel," Richard said. "Usually you have 45 minutes. She had to be running on fumes." He said his mom didn't even know how to drop the landing gear. Not only that, she was weak from two open-heart surgeries of her own and could hardly walk up steps, he said.

According to the *New York Times*, a local flying instructor flew beside Ms. Collins, coaching her on his radio. She approached the runway three times, hitting the tarmac hard on her third attempt before skidding to a halt with a collapsed nose wheel. Mr. Collins was pronounced dead at a local hospital, but Helen Collins walked away with minor injuries, *The Times* reported.

"She's an 80-year-old woman, but she's I guess what I would call a young 80-year-old woman," said the local airport director. "She's very spry, and to be in that situation and to be able to keep her cool the way she did is just amazing."

What extraordinary reserves of courage and resourcefulness lie within each of us just waiting to be released.

Here's another example, more low-key but just as meaningful. Newt Wallace, who is in his 90s, has walked the same blocks of downtown Winters, California since 1947 delivering the community's 2,300-circulation weekly newspaper.

"I don't hunt or play golf; I deliver papers," Wallace said in a recent interview as he walked his route. "I like delivering papers. I get to see the people I know." According to the story in the *New York Times*, Wallace spoke about delivering newspapers "the same way some people speak of a first love."

We only really grow old if – perish the thought – we retire from the fray prematurely, inviting unhappy thoughts to take up residence in our mind as we settle for the comfort of our customary habits and activities and our usual ways of seeing things.

Of course, there are many ways to experience meaning and express our love – as many ways as there are people. We don't all need to cross the Atlantic on a raft or land a plane in an emergency at a moment's notice.

For example, we can choose to slow down a bit and savor our moments more deeply – "to see a world in a grain of sand," as William Blake wrote, "and a Heaven in a Wild Flower." What did Walt

Whitman say? "I believe a leaf of grass is no less than the journey-work of the stars."

As long as we are alive, meaning will never be hidden or hard to find. We have been trained to think that we are flawed, sinful and worthless. But the reverse is true. We are spiritual beings with a magnificent gift to give and a unique destiny to fulfill.

It doesn't matter what the external circumstances of your life may be, whether you are young or old, whether you are well or unwell, whether you are filled with optimism or life seems murky and uncertain. As long as you are here, you are here for a reason. And the reason, I find, as I face the exigencies, joys and opportunities of each day, is very simple.

We are here to grow and expand. We are here to love life more deeply. We are here to see the world with new eyes, eyes of love and compassion. We are here to give the gift that only we can give.

Chapter 4

Changing Our Attitude toward Fear

"When you stop and open to what you have resisted throughout time, you find that fear is not fear. Fear is energy. Fear is space. Fear is the Buddha. It is Christ's heart knocking at your door."

– Gangaji

"Fear melts when you take action towards a goal you really want."

– Robert G. Allen

One of my most intense experiences of fear occurred when I was a child of 8. I lived with my mother on the 5th floor of an apartment block in London during the early days of the Second World War before being evacuated.

It was 1940 and Hitler had begun his daily bombing campaign – the Blitz – believing that by targeting civilians he could force Britain to surrender. Dad was away serving as a war correspondent when bombs fell in our immediate area one night.

I will never forget the terror I felt as our building began to sway to and fro in the blast and I clung to my mother for dear life. Nor will I ever forget how she kept saying, "It's all right, it's all right," as the bombs continued to fall. Where did she find the strength? She was right, though. No harm did come to us that terrifying night.

We all find our own ways of coming to terms with fear. For a long time – too long – I simply suppressed my feelings. I didn't realize it, mind you. But I erected a kind of cocoon around myself.

I can tell you with complete assurance it's not a good way of dealing with this particular issue. Sooner or later the fear that you are suppressing or trying to ignore will rise up and bite you.

How thankful I am to realize, with the gift of age, that it is possible to change our attitude to fear. We can learn to see this ancient enemy with eyes of compassion and love, as the spiritual teacher, Gangaji, suggests in her beautiful quote.

Our true nature is not fear. Our true nature is love – boundless, unchanging and forever free.

There is a natural law at work here, I find. As our love for what is true increases our fear decreases.

I am certainly not free of fear. Anxious feelings still arise. Perhaps none of us can be truly free of fear as long as we live in a fearful world. But as I become more conscious of a source of peace in myself that does not change and does not come and go, an underlying sense of calm deepens, and it is one of the most exciting experiences of my life.

I love the notion that fear – fearsome and threatening though it may appear at times – can actually help us heal if we stop resisting it and begin to see fear in a new light. Fear is lost energy that wants to come home. It is a friend who wants to help us become whole.

I love Robert Allen's wise message also. As I think about his words I remember that long-ago day when I awoke to find a brand new bike – my first bicycle – propped up in the hallway outside my bedroom.

It was my birthday. My heart swelled with pride as I hauled the bike out into the street. We lived at the top of a rise in a South London suburb called Petts Wood.

As I stood in the road with my bike ready to begin my first ride down the hill, only one thing marred that perfect moment – the little flutter of fear I felt as I looked down the gently sloping hill and reminded myself that I didn't know how to ride a bike.

But Robert Allen is right. As soon as I climbed on the bike and took off – albeit slowly – and with one or two accidents, for sure – fear began to simply melt away.

I'm so glad I overcame my fear that day because a few years later my parents upgraded me and gave me a beautiful blue bicycle with racing handlebars. Now my heart really soared. The bike brought me a sense of freedom I had never known before as I went on my first bicycle tour to Devon and Cornwall, travelling solo and staying at youth hostels.

Life is good. Life is good.

Chapter 5

Be Still and Know

"Learning how to be still, to really be still and let life happen – that stillness becomes a radiance."
                                        – Morgan Freeman

"Our spirit has an instinct for silence. Every soul innately yearns for stillness, for a space, a garden where we can till, reap, and rest, and by doing so come to a deeper sense of self and our place in the universe. Silence is not an absence but a presence. Not an emptiness but repletion. A filling up."
                                        – Anne D. LeClaire

I learned about the power of stillness many years ago while burning a pile of old, dead branches on a ranch in British Columbia. It was a hard lesson but an important one.

The meadow where I was working was surrounded by forest, and a haystack stood not far away. It was a warm, pleasant summer day, and I felt happy and at ease as I set fire to the tangle of brushwood.

Everything seemed to be going perfectly. But sometimes it's not good to become too relaxed. I looked up suddenly and realized with a profound shock that the fire that had seemed so peaceful and well-behaved was beginning to get out of hand.

A small circle of flames was spreading out in every direction. They weren't big flames but they were definitely on the move. I realized with horror that the fire would be quite capable of reaching the haystack and the forest too unless I could stop it.

I jumped up in a panic and began beating at the flames with my shovel, moving as quickly as I could around the ever-widening circle of fire.

I was putting out maximum effort, and at first, as I worked my way around the circle I imagined I was making progress. But then I looked back behind me and realized I was fooling myself. I only thought I had put the flames out. Small though they appeared to be, they were resilient and determined. As soon as I moved on, the flames simply sprang back to life behind me.

Now I really began to panic. I had never been in a situation like this in my life. I could end up being the cause of a dangerous forest fire.

Then I heard an inner voice say: "Be still. It's your only chance."

Although it seemed counter-intuitive, I followed the instruction. I stopped my frantic activity and stood still for a moment. I realized I had to change my approach and proceed in a calm, methodical way, making sure each fiery little flame was well and truly extinguished before I moved on.

It took some self-discipline, but that is what I did. I ignored whatever was going on in the larger circle of flames and focused my entire attention on the little patch of fire immediately in front of me, making sure those flames were out before I moved further on around the circle. God was kind to me that day. It seemed to take forever. But the moment came when I stood up, looked around, and realized with immense relief that all the flames were out.

I figured I had done enough work for one day. I went to the local café, ordered two chocolate milk shakes, and thanked my lucky stars everything had turned out okay.

I have never forgotten the lesson I learned that day on a ranch in British Columbia. Are you in a difficult situation? Does a challenge loom before you? Be still, and you will know what to do. The ancient words of Psalm 46:10 are true today: "Be still, and know that I am God."

Chapter 6

One Thing Between
You and Your Dream

*"We all have the extraordinary coded within us,
waiting to be released."*

– Jean Houston

*"You are a child of God. Your playing small does not
serve the world. There is nothing enlightened about
shrinking so that other people won't feel insecure
around you. We are all meant to shine, as children
do."*

– Marianne Williamson

Only one thing stands between you and the
beautiful fulfillment that is your true destiny. It's
the toxic belief inhaled from the very atmosphere
around you when you were young that you are
somehow flawed and imperfect.

The world got its hooks into you at an early
age, a very early age, and there was nothing you
could do about it. You were just a child, for
heaven's sake. There was nothing you could do to

protect yourself from this monstrous lie. There was no way you could sort out for yourself what was true and what wasn't true.

As the light of innocence and joy began to fade from your eyes, the sense of greatness that was with you when you first arrived on planet earth also began to fade. You succumbed to the insidious notion that nothing you do is quite good enough.

An entire culture – an entire way of living, or perhaps I should say dying – has been constructed out of this perverted notion that we are somehow irretrievably flawed.

Sure, we all have our foibles, our human nature characteristics. For example, I'm a "quick reactor," as my wife puts it. Sometimes strong feelings and strong opinions brew up in me quite quickly.

But a wonderful truth waits to be revealed more fully in you and me. Our true nature is not sinful. It is perfect. It is happy. It is free. It is untouched by our weaknesses and untroubled by any of the feelings that arise in us, sometimes pleasant, sometimes not.

As I've mentioned before, we are not the miserable creatures the world would have us believe. We do need to acknowledge our flaws and pretenses, of course. But this is one of the great opportunities of aging – the opportunity to change our ways or even change our mind from time to time. It's okay. It adds to the fun.

I know of no more encouraging truth than this. The greatness that you and I sensed as a child is with us still. It has gone nowhere. It is our birthright, beautifully described by William Wordsworth in his poem, Intimations of Immortality: "Not in entire forgetfulness/And not in utter nakedness/But trailing clouds of glory do we come/From God, who is our home."

The world waits with outstretched arms for the gift only you can bring.

Chapter 7

How I Made Peace with Death

"Ultimately, none of us are orphans. We are all in the position I was, in that we have other family: beings who are watching and looking out for us – beings we have momentarily forgotten, but who, if we open ourselves to their presence, are waiting to help us navigate our time here on earth."

– Eben Alexander, M.D.

"Begin to see yourself as a soul with a body rather than a body with a soul."

– Wayne Dyer

Some people think that death is the end of everything. But I am not one of those people. And the reason – one of the reasons anyway, a very special reason – has to do with Joy, my wife of 25 years, who died suddenly on December 15, 1991.

We were married in a spiritual community in the interior of British Columbia in 1967 and lived there until she died. It was an extraordinary life, a wonderful adventure, sharing with perhaps 100 other kindred spirits in a mutual love of integrity and truth. We had a son, we followed the call of truth, we created a newsletter called *Integrity* that

opened friendships all over the world, and we made nine visits to India.

And then one day – who could have imagined such a thing? – Life plucked Joy from me.

We were flying home to Vancouver, British

The author with Joy

Columbia after celebrating our 25th anniversary in the Caribbean, when Joy moved to the rear of the plane, saying she had a headache and wanted more room.

Perhaps half-an-hour later the terrifying moment arrived when a stewardess stopped beside me and said my wife didn't look well, and would I please take a look at her. I sat beside Joy but soon realized she was not really present anymore. I tried again and again to reach her, to speak to her, but there was no recognition in her eyes.

She had such a lovely face. Such a lovely smile. But soon I would see them no more. When we reached Vancouver, Joy was rushed to Richmond General Hospital, where a doctor, very grave, summoned me to his office. She had suffered a fatal aneurysm and there was nothing they could do to help her. "You must make peace with yourself as best you can," the doctor told me.

I was numb from head to toe. I sat with Joy for about four hours before she died. Here's the strange thing: every now and again she would turn her head and look at me. And I swear that more than once she winked at me.

Then came a moment like sun breaking through a cloud. I sensed she wanted to say something, and as I bent my head toward her, I heard her whisper, soft as a piece of silk falling to the floor, "Home." It was just one word but it is a word I have never forgotten.

I wondered for a moment if she meant she wanted to be taken back to our village in the interior of British Columbia. But then I knew that wasn't it at all. She was reaching out to me one last time to let me know she was on her way to Heaven and all was well.

I am so thankful for my last moments with Joy. I often feel her presence with me as I continue with my life and I feel her blessing with me now.

Chapter 8

Hold Your Head High

"If you have integrity, nothing else matters. If you don't have integrity, nothing else matters."
– Alan Simpson

"The hero in each of us is required to answer the call of individuation. We must turn away from the cacophony of the outer world to hear the inner voice. When we can dare to live its promptings, then we achieve personhood."
– James Hollis

"Nothing is at last sacred but the integrity of your own mind," declared Emerson. I have found that when I listen to my inner voice and live by its promptings, as Dr. Hollis suggests, my life isn't always comfortable, but it leads – with a few twists and turns, mind you – toward increasing freedom and happiness.

Life unfolds in remarkable ways that I could never have imagined if I had not followed that quiet voice in my heart. And I realize that the universe is not my enemy but is my ally and friend.

My father, Reginald Foster, had integrity, and it was just as well, because the time came when that was about all he had to rely on. At the age of 61, Dad, a veteran London journalist, found himself at the center of a whirlwind concerning stories he and another reporter had written about a British spy named Vassall.

The government set up a tribunal to investigate these leaks, and my father and a colleague were given an ultimatum. "Tell us who gave you the information for your stories or you'll go to prison," said the judge.

Was Dad going to succumb to the intense pressure? Or be true to the journalistic ethics instilled in him since he became a reporter on the London *Daily Mail* at age 19, and refuse to disclose his source?

In a dramatic face-off in a crowded, hushed chamber, Dad politely told the judge he was sorry but he couldn't do what the judge wanted. To do so would be untrue not only to himself but to many brave colleagues who had perished in WWII, he said.

So Dad was sent to prison for six months, and he and his colleague became known throughout Britain and beyond as "the silent reporters."

We never know when we may be called upon to make a similar choice – to be true to ourselves and our principles, or not. The circumstances may not be as dramatic as the situation involving my father. But does it make any difference, really, whether the issues are "important" or not in a worldly sense?

There have been times in my relationship with my wife, JoAnn, for example, when I felt I needed to share something with her even though I didn't have to, and it might be embarrassing. A little voice inside me said it was the right thing to do. What can we do but trust that inner voice – trust that if we are true to our integrity everything will work out as it should.

Dad wasn't trying to be a hero or impress anyone when he stood up and spoke to the judge as he did. He realized that he didn't really have a choice.

Without integrity, our lives become hollow. We are a house divided, as Abraham Lincoln said. Our lives may glitter on the outside, but true meaning and happiness continually elude us.

What a different story when integrity is present. When we surrender the delusion of choice, so that all that matters to us in any moment is to express what is true, right, and helpful as best we may, we find a source of strength and comfort within ourselves that never fails.

Actually, things worked out quite well for Dad. He was sent to an "open" prison where he became good friends with a number of inmates and with the warden. He helped to organize sports and other activities. And his health improved, too, with the regular meals and exercise and a significant decrease in his consumption of beer. British reporters do so love their pubs and their beer.

I thought of my father some years ago when I sat down and wrote a short poem about character. I'd love to share it with you.

Character

An ancient song stirs in my memory
like wildflowers shouting
on a hill, and it says:
"Not a leaf astir upon the tree,
Not a ripple on the surface
of the shining pool.
Silence is the cornerstone
of true character."
I guess the mountain thinks so
as it breathes out its majesty with every breath,
and the prairie also,
stretching forever beyond gray city walls.
Yet there are times
when silence is not true character,
and life makes a strong wind blow
on the prairie or in the human heart.
It demands that a human mouth speak,
maybe yours, maybe mine,
and say the thing that must be said
if truth and love and kindness are to have their way.
What is it,
this thing called character?

Only my heart knows,
as it turns to a light so close
and yet so illimitable
I'm not sure it really has a name.

Chapter 9

How to Boost Your Confidence

"When we least expect it, life sets us a challenge to test our courage and willingness to change; at such a moment, there is no point in pretending that nothing has happened or in saying that we are not yet ready. The challenge will not wait. Life does not look back. A week is more than enough time for us to decide whether or not to accept our destiny."
– Paulo Coelho

"Our attitude in the face of life's challenges determines our suffering or our freedom."
– Tara Brach

I discovered the truth of Paulo Coelho's words first-hand when I bought a beautiful new computer one day. Just as Paulo says, I was immediately faced with a challenge that wouldn't wait.

I brought my new computer home and began trying to get it working, but realized right away I was in over my head. Computers are not my strong point, to put it mildly. I'm an artistic fellow, more at home working on a poem than penetrating the mysteries of a computer.

But I'm here to say I'm so happy that computers do exist and are part of my world. They make my life so much richer, fuller, and more interesting. Computers didn't exist when Dad was churning out stories for his newspaper on a battered old typewriter. But now they do exist. And they help me connect with people near and far, give my gift and create new products in a way that is truly magical.

I was prompted to buy a new computer because my old one was 10 years old and like an old dog, or a beloved pet, it was getting harder and harder for it to move at all. It was time for something new. But what to buy? What make? What model? Just trying to decide these questions was challenging enough.

But that was just the beginning. There was a new version of *Word* to understand, along with a new version of *Windows*. There were various new programs and updates to old programs to install. Many times I thought I had everything set up properly, only to discover there was another piece I hadn't even thought of yet. And so it went. One challenge after another.

But here's what I want to share with you. As I sit here this morning, working on my new computer, I'm filled with much joy because this challenge has boosted my confidence. I realize more strongly than ever that life really does want us to expand our boundaries, regardless of our age. It wants us to keep creating a more fulfilling, happy life for ourselves and our world no matter what.

Using this computer is like driving down the road in a Cadillac (not that I've ever done that, mind you) compared to riding in the back of a battered old pickup.

And so it comes down to this. Life is good. Life is sweet. Life really does want to bless us, and lead us to a richer, more abundant experience. But we have to play our part. We have to keep listening to the wisdom of our own heart. We have to keep moving forward even though part of us may want to quit, or we wonder, "Can I really do this?" or "Is it really worth it?"

We have to be flexible, willing to change our minds every now and again and go in a new direction if need be. But most of all – we have to keep trusting our own unconquerable spirit.

I'm happy to share these thoughts with you sitting in front of my new computer. And I'm thankful for the people who made this beautiful machine and for the technicians who helped me get my new computer up and running.

No man is an island, wrote the poet John Donne. Whatever challenges life may bring we need each other, that's for sure.

Chapter 10

The Blessings of Aging

"It's very simple. As you grow, you learn more. If you stayed at twenty-two, you'd always be as ignorant as you were at twenty-two. Aging is not just decay, you know. It's growth. It's more than the negative that you're going to die, it's also the positive that you understand you're going to die, and that you live a better life because of it."

— Mitch Albom

"Every day I feel is a blessing from God. And I consider it a new beginning. Yeah, everything is beautiful."

— Prince

I was finishing up my routine at the gym when a young fellow came over to me. He had a friendly smile on his face as he looked at me.

"How old are you?" he asked in a simple, straightforward way. More directly I'm sure than would have happened in the Britain of my youth.

I had never met this man but smiled back and told him my age. He positively beamed and said how happy he was to realize we don't have to go downhill as we age but can stay vigorous and active.

It was a brief conversation, but it made me think how despite its challenges aging can be a time of remarkable blessing.

I was delighted last evening when I saw a clip on the evening news of a good-looking 89-year-old man being honored at a graduation ceremony at an American university. How happy and proud he looked, and he deserved to be happy and proud.

Every life is unique. But here are some ways in which I experience greater joy and fulfillment in life.

Aging, I find, makes possible the fulfillment of a dream that has been with me since my youth, the dream of knowing myself more fully and becoming more free in myself.

My appreciation for the magic of little moments is increasing. I realize that if we are already happy, it takes a very small thing to make us happier – watching a bird in flight, for example, or saying hello to the person who is serving us in a coffee shop.

My love for people is increasing, not diminishing. "Everyone's doing their best," I remind myself if impatience comes to visit, which of course it does. Perhaps it's because I'm not in such a hurry. Or maybe it's because the passing years and a whole lot of pain have made me more capable of empathy and compassion.

I have always loved Nature, and the lessons she teaches. But I honor her more each day for the gifts she gives so generously. We have a creek just below our townhome complex that flows all year long. I never tire of listening to its sweet sounds as it swirls skillfully past rocks and other obstacles.

I see the past traumas of my life in a new light. I used to think they were terrible and unjust, but now I realize they actually opened a door to greater freedom and happiness.

My love for my wife, JoAnn, deepens. Every day I appreciate her strong, caring spirit and wonder how I could be so lucky. Except I don't think it is luck, really. I think a hand of grace brought us together and keeps us together.

Age brings the opportunity to forgive if forgiveness is needed. For example, I see my father in a new light. I neither understood him nor liked him, really, when he lived. Now I see him for the brave, remarkable man he truly was.

I feel his love blessing me as I continue my earthly journey. I am so thankful for him, and for my wonderful mother and all the members of my family who have departed this realm. I feel their presence and love and I am grateful for each of them.

Chapter 11

Sometimes Simple and Familiar Is Good

"The little things? The little moments? They aren't little."

– Jon Kabat-Zinn

"Each day is an adventure in discovering the meaning of life. It is each little thing that you do that day – whether it be spending time with your friends, running in a cross-country meet or just simply staring at the crashing ocean – that holds the key to discovering the meaning of life. I would rather be out enjoying these things than pondering them."

– Jack Canfield

I was feeling two conflicting emotions at the same time this particular morning. Does that ever happen to you? The adventurous side of me, which worries sometimes that it isn't getting enough expression in my life, was saying, "Look, it's Sunday, and you've been working hard this week.

Do something bold like going for a hike in the mountains so you know you're really alive."

But another part of me wasn't so sure. It just didn't seem to want to do anything too exciting or dramatic at all. I went and sat for a few minutes with JoAnn, always a good idea if I need a little help clarifying my mind about something.

She was working on a new sewing project, and of course said, as she always does, that I must decide for myself what to do. But she suggested that the past few days had been particularly exciting and challenging for me – working on a new book project that could possibly make a difference to our lives if it all works out – and perhaps what I really needed was simply to relax and let things settle down a bit.

I decided to gas up the car, a fairly safe step. But then, as I finished filling up the tank, I thought to myself, "Why not just go for a walk by the creek and be nourished and soothed by something simple that won't need a lot of exertion?"

So I drove home, walked down the little hill at the back of our property and sat down on a bench to listen to the sweet sound of the creek. In just a few moments a chickadee – one of my favorite birds – began to sing, and I saw a blue jay, the first one I've seen this year.

I met friendly people. I met friendly dogs. I sat on a rock beside a small waterfall. I saw daffodils getting ready to bloom. It was a simple little adventure. And yet I knew it was just right. It was what I needed to do.

I felt fulfilled, and rested. I felt nourished.

Sometimes life demands that we be bold, and daring, and take a huge step into the unknown regardless of any uncertainty or anxiety we may feel, and no matter what the cost may be. There is no guarantee at all things will work out the way we hope they will – but we sense deep in our bones that our very destiny is at stake.

And sometimes simple and familiar is good. Oh, so good. May we have the wisdom to know what really needs to be done in any situation, and may our lives prosper because of it.

Chapter 12

Something Calling to You

"After a time I found that I could almost listen to the silence which had a dimension all of its own. I started to attend to its strange and beautiful texture, which, of course, it was impossible to express in words."
— Karen Armstrong

"It's important to be heroic, ambitious, productive, efficient, creative, and progressive, but these qualities don't necessarily nurture soul. The soul has different concerns, of equal value: downtime for reflection, conversation, and reverie; beauty that is captivating and pleasuring; relatedness to the environs and to people; and any animal's rhythm of rest and activity."
— Thomas Moore

There is something in you and me that is not troubled in the least by the various challenges and upheavals of our lives. No matter what has happened to you – or is happening to you now – it is untouched and unharmed by any of it.

Good times come and good times go. You meet someone who makes your life complete, or maybe you lose someone you loved with a passion. You achieve a dream you were following for many years, or perhaps you wake up one morning and realize your life is empty and always has been.

But this silent presence within you is unmoved by any of it. It shines like the sun. It's at peace. It doesn't move; it doesn't change. It's not going somewhere, and it didn't come from somewhere either. It's like a seed planted in the earth, waiting to be born into a flower or a tree, or a new world. And the only word I can think to describe it is love.

This love that is in us was never born, and will never die. It is the source of everything, but here's the interesting thing. It has never once lost its faith in you. It knows why you are here, and amid all the trials and tribulations of your life, it has never once deviated in its love for you.

Shh. Be still. Listen. Can you hear something calling to you amid the hustle and bustle of your daily routine? It's love, your own true nature, and it wants to be free. It wants you to be free too. It wants to come out of hiding and set the whole world free.

Its time has come and it's on the move. It has its own agenda for this world and it doesn't really care about our political, cultural or religious persuasions. It is love, and you'd better believe it is not going to be defeated.

Chapter 13

Never Stop Growing and Changing

"The capacity for growth depends on one's ability to internalize and to take personal responsibility. If we forever see our life as a problem caused by others, a problem to be 'solved,' then no change will occur."
— James Hollis

"If we don't change, we don't grow. If we don't grow, we aren't really living."
— Gail Sheehy

Life has a law we need to follow if we want to age with wisdom and joy. The law reads like this: "Never stop changing and growing." The trouble is we are sometimes tempted to ignore this law in favor of the supposed comfort of the status quo.

I've been going to a gym for about 10 years. It's a lifesaver in many ways. The other day, a trainer came over to me as I was working on the leg press machine and asked if I'd be interested in changing my routine so as to challenge my body and give it a chance to grow some new lean muscle.

I liked the theory part of it. Some nice new muscle sounded great. But then came the first session with the trainer and – horrors – new exercises I had never done before.

For example, the trainer, Peggy, asked me to stand with my back to the wall, a large medicine ball nestled behind me on top of my butt, and then extend my feet, bend my legs and slide up and down the wall with the ball supporting me from behind. It felt a little weird, to be honest. I wasn't sure I liked it. And I worried that my feet might somehow slip forward and I'd land with a big bump on my rear end.

The gym is a large facility, and Peggy led me through several other new challenges and procedures. I realize, as I sit at my computer this morning, my muscles calm at last, that my old routine is probably gone forever.

I loved my previous workout too. I knew exactly what to expect. My body knew exactly what to expect. I didn't have to think. I didn't have to change. I strutted around the gym with the familiarity and nonchalance of a pro, proud of myself because I was actually lifting quite a bit of weight.

There is a place for familiar routines, of course. But if life says it's time to change, what else can we do but change?

Chapter 14

One Step at a Time

"Adversity is a natural part of being human. It is the height of arrogance to prescribe a moral code or health regime or spiritual practice as an amulet to keep things from falling apart. Things do fall apart. It is in their nature to do so. When we try to protect ourselves from the inevitability of change, we are not listening to the soul."

– Elizabeth Lesser

"If your emotional abilities aren't in hand, if you don't have self-awareness, if you are not able to manage your distressing emotions, if you can't have empathy and have effective relationships, then no matter how smart you are, you are not going to get very far."

– Daniel Goleman

One step at a time. It's a law of nature. No matter how challenging a situation may seem to be, there is always a baby step we can take that will generate some momentum and, if we take it, make it possible for us to see what our next step is, and the next.

My wife and I have built a life together that we love and that is a true boon to each of us in our latter years. But it began, like anything truly worthwhile, as a tiny seed, and has taken countless small steps to reach the place where we are now.

When we first become aware of each other, JoAnn lived in Denver, and I lived like a hermit in a seniors' apartment block in Vancouver, British Columbia. I was in my 60s and in a complete funk about what to do with my life following the collapse of the spiritual community that had been my home for 36 years.

We met each other at a retreat, and soon afterwards, began a long-distance relationship. It was interesting, it was challenging, and it was, as I say, one baby step after another. We went for a holiday in Hawaii and it worked out okay, except that JoAnn tried to drink all the champagne the first night. A bit later on, we went to the UK to visit my dad, then in his 90s. That worked out okay too, except for the time when JoAnn tried to help out in his kitchen, which caused a terrible fuss.

Eventually, we became even bolder and decided we wanted to live together. But I didn't want to come to the U.S. illegally and JoAnn didn't want to move to Canada for various reasons.

We were in a situation so many people have experienced. Finally JoAnn offered to sponsor me for a temporary visa that would allow me to move to Denver and live with her for 60 days – at the end of which time we would either need to get married or I would need to return to Canada pronto.

We had progressed quite well in our relationship, but what we were talking about now was a BIG step. It wasn't a baby step at all. I remember talking with a friend who shook his head and warned, "It sounds drastic, Chris."

I had to agree with him. It was drastic, as real change usually is. I had already lost so much that was familiar and that had given me security and a sense of home, such as the community in which I had lived, and my wife Joy. There was also the simple fact that I had lived in British Columbia for 40 years. If I moved to America I would lose the last of my "roots" – wouldn't I?

But on the other hand, it might open a door to a remarkable new life I couldn't even imagine …yet.

I agonized about it, and then one day I decided, "Why not at least apply for the entry visa? There's no harm in that. See what happens. They may not even want you in the country." It was a baby step – but a manageable one.

JoAnn, of course, had also wrestled with what was a very big step for her too. After all, she was being asked to open up her home to someone she didn't know all THAT well yet. She was being asked to share her precious resources, and she also had to satisfy the authorities that she could and would sponsor me.

But it works. It really does. One step at a time. It's Nature's way, and it will bring you through virtually anything life may throw at you.

Chapter 15

Have You Changed
Your Mind Lately?

*"Begin challenging your own assumptions. Your
assumptions are your windows on the world. Scrub
them off every once in a while, or the light won't come
in."*

– Alan Alda

*"I rise to taste the dawn, and find that love alone will
shine today."*

– Ken Wilber

Sometimes we age prematurely and imprison the
joy that would keep us young by adopting rigid
opinions and prejudices about this or that.
Perhaps we see it as a sign of weakness to change
our opinions. Perhaps we are frightened of change.

Obviously, there are times when changing your
mind isn't appropriate. I'm glad, for instance, that
the British people refused to back down when
faced with the preening might of Nazi Germany.
But being able to change our minds when

appropriate is crucial to our happiness, success, fulfillment, and of course, relationships. Sometimes, after all, our initial impression of a person or situation isn't accurate at all.

A year or so ago, I decided to check out a church located near my home. I'm not religious, particularly, but I am spiritual. I was interested, too, in the possibility of finding some kindred spirits and making new friends. So I drove over to investigate this church one Sunday morning, and was immediately put off by the fact that it was apparently housed in the corner of a large business building.

"It doesn't look like a proper church," I thought, with mild annoyance, as I went inside. The proceedings had already begun, so with no one to say hello to me, I took a seat at the back to do some more investigating. A man was playing on a small piano, and a woman was singing some songs, but again, it seemed kind of hokey to me. I wasn't impressed.

Perhaps you can see a pattern unfolding here. In any case, the minister, who was a woman, stepped to the podium and began to speak. Now I'll be able to get a feel of things, I thought. The woman began by telling a story. I usually enjoy stories, but for some reason I didn't find this one very interesting. After a few minutes I decided this wasn't the right place for me, and without further ado, I got up and quietly left the hall.

Bear with me, please, as I bring you up to date.

Recently, I remembered the little church I had visited once with such disappointing results. "You should go and visit there again," a little voice said in my heart. "You might really like it. You may have been a bit hasty and jumped to a conclusion when you went there before."

I try to listen to my inner nudges. It's true, I thought to myself. I may have written off the church, and more importantly, the people who meet there, prematurely. I didn't put on a tie, but I put on my nice sports jacket and drove to the church.

It was a wonderful visit. I was so glad I had changed my mind. At the door, as I entered, three women waited to greet arrivals. I caught the eye of the nearest greeter, an older woman, and I thought, as I shook her hand and smiled at her, "What a delightful person. I feel at home already."

Exactly the same man was playing the piano. Exactly the same woman was singing. But it all sounded quite different this time.

As I listened to the speaker I realized she had a lot of wisdom to share and I could and would enjoy listening to her.

Things just kept on getting better and better. I like people, so I hung around after the service for a coffee and chat. I love sailing, and the first person I started chatting with had just been sailing in San Francisco Bay. I met a friendly member of the church board who told me all about her daughter, an adventurous 49-year-old currently teaching in Africa.

My Sunday morning visit to a local church was all I could have hoped for and then some. One of my new friends even gave me a carnation to give to my wife, which I presented proudly to JoAnn when I got home. Good move. I got some extra brownie points without even really trying.

As far as I'm concerned, it's one of life's most precious gifts – the ability to change our minds when it seems appropriate.

Part Two

Joy

Chapter 16

Invitation to Joy

"It can take a while before we begin to realize that retirement really plunges us into joy. But if we decide to live this new, unscripted time with joy, then life will come pouring into us, almost more fully than we can sometimes bear."

— Joan Chittister

"In my own worst seasons I've come back from the colorless world of despair by forcing myself to look hard, for a long time, at a single glorious thing: a flame of red geranium outside my bedroom window. And then another: my daughter in a yellow dress. And another: the perfect outline of a full, dark sphere behind the crescent moon. Until I learned to be in love with my life again."

— Barbara Kingsolver

I don't think it's useful to try to define the word "joy". It may be true, for example, that joy is a reminder of our heavenly origin, or our oneness with creation, but what does that tell us? Joy is free. It is not something that you can catch in a butterfly net, so to speak, and add to your collection. You can't order up a serving of joy like you can order up a gourmet meal in a restaurant.

But we can experience joy. That's the good news here. And when we do experience joy then our lives have meaning and they bless the world of which we are a part.

I stepped outside our front door a few moments ago and stood on the porch of our townhouse to listen to a bird singing close by. It was just a small bird, perhaps a finch of some kind, but my, how beautifully it could sing. It went on and on. Talk about joy in expression. I realized the bird had chosen to alight at the very top of the large blue spruce tree that grows near our front door.

I realized, also, that the bird was not alone. After it had sung for a little while it would pause for a moment, and I would hear another bird begin to sing, as if in response. They kept this up for quite a while, singing to each other – and of course, to me.

I sometimes think that when we come to the end of our lives, it won't necessarily be our great accomplishments that will loom large in our memory. What we will cherish most may be those simple moments in which we experienced a sense of oneness with the wondrous universe of which we are part.

Soon after moving to British Columbia in 1955 I bought a 22-foot sailboat. It had a small cabin and a 4hp inboard engine. Life was a continual challenge for the little motor, perhaps because it was getting on in years, or perhaps because it had not been installed properly, and sat at a rather odd angle in the bottom of the boat. I was never quite sure if it would be able to rise to the occasion and do its job or not.

I named my boat "Vision," because it was the promise of a new land filled with giant forests and mountains that had drawn me to British Columbia. Despite the objections of my parents, I longed for freedom and open spaces. I read Robert Service and Walt Whitman every day, and rebelled at life in the busy streets of London.

While working as a junior reporter in Fleet Street I had sailed a 16-foot sailboat on a river in Essex, but I had never done any coastal sailing. So it was an excited but inexperienced young sailor who set out one spring day from Victoria on a cruise through the Gulf Islands.

The weather was sunny and warm, and for a while everything was great. The water was blue, the sky was blue, and I sang happily to myself as I sailed along. And then suddenly – because of poor planning on my part, no doubt – I found myself in a difficult and intense situation as I tried to navigate through a narrow passage against a strong rip-tide that treated my little boat with utmost derision.

Sometimes I thought I was making headway, but then I would look at the nearby shore and think I was standing still. As my motor sputtered away and the water swirled viciously around me, I noticed small whirlpools here and there which added to my worry.

"It's all right," I kept saying to myself, a favorite mantra when I am in trouble. "It's all right."

Adding to the excitement, a strong, gusty wind began to blow. I kept looking nervously at the engine, wondering if it would be able to bring me through the rough, chaotic currents. But it did. It was magnificent. It hesitated a tad now and again, but it kept on going.

After what seemed like hours I emerged at last into open water, and a little later reached the entrance of a beautiful cove. Again, I hadn't planned this. But talk about a change of pace. Now I was surrounded by soft evening air and a stillness that was palpable. There was not another boat in sight as with just a whisper of a breeze I ghosted across the velvet surface of the sea.

It was a wide, spacious cove and as I floated across the water in a pool of total silence, I felt God's presence with me most keenly. The tree-lined shore all around me was a friendly, protective presence and I felt at one with everything. I was one with the water, the land, the sky, and the odd star that peeped out to say hello.

More than fifty years have passed since I sailed out of Victoria harbor to begin my first cruise. But the joy and peace of that memorable evening is with me still as I peck away at my keyboard, doing my best to give my gift and complete my latest book.

Joy is our birthright. Robert Browning had it right: "God's in his heaven – All's right with the world."

Chapter 17

The Simple Pleasures of Life

"A morning-glory at my window satisfies me more than the metaphysics of books."
            – Walt Whitman

"Our life before moving to Washington was filled with simple joys...Saturdays at soccer games, Sundays at grandma's house...and a date night for Barack and me was either dinner or a movie, because as an exhausted mom, I couldn't stay awake for both."
            – Michelle Obama

I have a theory that goes something like this. The more we appreciate the simple pleasures of life the more balanced our lives become, and the stronger and happier we become.

I'm going to use a dog named Kato as an example. Kato is a St. Bernard who lives in the same townhome complex in which JoAnn and I live. He's getting on in years, is about the size of a small pony and is one of my best friends without a doubt.

For various reasons, JoAnn and I don't own a dog. So I enjoy, and love other people's dogs – Kato especially. We seem to have a special bond. Early this morning I was sitting in my chair eating my porridge when I heard JoAnn call out: "I think Kato and Debbie are coming around the corner."

I put down my bowl, open the front door, and sure enough there is Kato straining at the leash, slobbering with excitement, and anxious to see me.

As Debbie keeps a firm grip on the leash I grab hold of my four-legged friend. I take his large head in my hands and tell him how beautiful he is. I grab hold of his body and give him a hug and he rears his head in pleasure.

I'm not an expert in animal behavior. But I do know this. Love speaks in any language – and just as I feel Kato's love, and am blessed by it, so I am sure this aging, magnificent creature is blessed also.

There is so much more to life than the hustle and bustle that waits to consume us every day with its complexities and challenges. The simplest moment has a gift to give that can transform our experience if we are open to see and receive that gift.

Following my visit with my four-legged friend, JoAnn and I went for a walk near our property. The morning air was like chilled champagne. The deep blue Colorado sky was pristine, not a cloud in sight.

We passed a mallard duck standing all alone on a grassy area some distance from the creek that flows year-round, even though it is named Dry Creek for some strange reason. The duck looked a bit lost, like he wasn't quite sure what to do. I don't only enjoy communing with dogs; I enjoy communing with ducks too, so there was another simple pleasure waiting for us. Incidentally, we didn't see the duck on our return, so I'm guessing he found his way to the creek okay.

We've had rain recently, and the greenery that awaited us along the banks of the creek was overwhelming. A robin was in full throttle, and ravens, chickadees and songbirds joined in the concert. Soon we came to my favorite spot where stepping stones provide a bridge across the creek. I enjoyed – for what, the hundredth time? The thousandth time? – standing on a rock in the middle of the stream listening to its sweet melody.

I love watching this stream and the way the water flows so easily and effortlessly around the rocks. The water isn't troubled by the rocks at all. It doesn't get into a battle with them. It simply swirls around them and keeps on going.

The water reminds me of the truth that flows in each of us from its invisible source and is also well capable of navigating any of the challenges that may come our way.

Chapter 18

The Secret Bliss of Aging

"Follow your bliss and the universe will open doors where there were only walls."
— Joseph Campbell

"When you recover or discover something that nourishes your soul and brings joy, care enough about yourself to make room for it in your life."
— Jean Shinoda Bolen

Aging has a poor reputation, no doubt. As Linda Fried, of the International Longevity Center at Columbia University, put it in an article I read recently, "We have such a human aversion to getting old; it's associated with death, and death is scary."

But big changes are happening in our approach to aging. More and more people are realizing that growing older doesn't mean you have to become "old" – and we can follow our bliss at any age.

Take Margaret Hagerty, for example. She's a remarkable 88-year-old who started running at age 64 and has since become a world-famous international marathon runner. She is listed in the Guinness World Records as "the oldest person to complete a marathon on each of the 7 continents at age 81." Margaret was quoted one time as saying: "You do not know what is possible until you try the impossible and make a hard fought effort to succeed. You will be amazed at what you can achieve."

Our world is obviously in a pile of trouble right now. But how encouraging it is to see and know that not all the change that is transpiring is bad. Barriers are being broken down and new possibilities are emerging in so many ways – including the way we choose to see and experience aging.

In my own life, for example, painful feelings still arise, challenges still arise, and aging takes its toll in various ways. But always present, sometimes in the background and sometimes in the foreground is a growing awareness of the pure, undiluted joy of being that is surely the "holy grail" for which we all seek.

Joy. It is our birthright, isn't it? Yes, it can seem elusive at times. Yet the older I become the more clearly I see that joy itself is actually always present. We just have to learn to become more conscious of its presence. We have to learn to see joy in little moments, for example – and perhaps difficult moments.

Is it possible to be joyful sitting in a dentist's chair? I think it is. Let us become hunters, not so much of outer riches, though surely there is nothing wrong with outer riches – but of joy.

I love the words of Joan Chittister, author of a wonderful book on aging entitled *The Gift of Years*:

"The slate is clean. The days are ours. The task now is to learn how to live again. We can decide to live with joy. Or we can allow ourselves to live looking back with bitterness."

I've already mentioned a large, gorgeous blue spruce tree that grows quite close to our front door. I look at this tree every day, admiring its grace, looking for any creatures that may be finding shelter in its branches. I can state with conviction that no bitterness emanates from this noble creation. As far as I am concerned, the tree brings only joy.

I take to heart every day Jean Shinoda Bolen's beautiful advice. I am thankful for the joy my blue spruce tree brings to me – and make sure there is room in my life to receive that joy.

Chapter 19

The Buoyant Spirit

"The human capacity for burden is like bamboo – far more flexible than you'd ever believe at first glance."
— Jodi Picoult

"You may encounter many defeats, but you must not be defeated. In fact, it may be necessary to encounter the defeats, so you can know who you are, what you can rise from, how you can still come out of it."
— Maya Angelou

The Collins English Dictionary defines *buoyancy* in four ways:

1. The ability to float in a liquid or to rise in a fluid.

2. (Physics) the property of a fluid to exert an upward force on a body that is wholly or partly submerged in it.

3. The ability to recover quickly after setback; resilience.

4. Cheerfulness.

One of the most dismal days of my life was the day when my primary care doctor, worried how thin and weak I had become, sent me to hospital by ambulance for further examination. I had to go through various tests and then a psychiatrist came to see me in the emergency ward, and we chatted for a while.

I thought we had quite a good chat, although it troubled me that a uniformed guard with a pistol on his belt was sitting in a chair in the hallway outside my cubicle, looking at me. What was that all about? Did it have anything to do with me? Did he think I might try to damage myself?

After she had chatted with me for a while, the psychiatrist left my little cubicle and went to look for my wife, who was waiting further down the hall.

"She told me you were in a clinical depression but she simply couldn't understand why you were so cheerful and had such a buoyant spirit," JoAnn told me later.

I am so thankful for the buoyant spirit that is the birthright of each one of us, waiting to help us and lift us up even in our darkest times. As the Spanish nun and mystic, St. Teresa of Avila so beautifully declared: "Let nothing disturb thee; Let nothing dismay thee; All things pass; God changeth never."

Chapter 20

Is Happiness Hiding in Plain Sight?

"We are very good at preparing to live, but not very good at living. We know how to sacrifice ten years for a diploma and we are willing to work very hard to get a job, a car, a house, and so on. But we have difficulty remembering that we are alive in the present moment, the only moment there is for us to be alive."
— Thich Nhat Hanh

"If your happiness depends on what somebody else does, I guess you do have a problem."
— Richard Bach

Every once in a while, in my exchanges with my wife, I succeed in saying something that is funny – funny enough anyway to provoke spontaneous laughter in her.

I've noticed how at a certain point, when she has been laughing awhile, she pauses and says, "Oh heck." It's been going on for years. I realize how much I love hearing these two simple little words in this context.

I've also become more consciously aware of something else that happens when she laughs. She always finishes her laugh with a warble – don't know how else to describe it – a unique

sound that comes from somewhere deep in her throat and sounds like happiness itself humming with joy.

JoAnn and her devoted hubby

I shared a joke with my doctor one time. We were talking on the phone, and he was apologizing for the fact that he was croaking because of a bad cold.

As the conversation came to a close I couldn't resist it. I said, "I've got one or two good medical books here, Dr. Thom. Maybe I could find some advice that would help with your cold?"

I'm afraid my jokes don't always work. But I think this one did, because he began wheezing with laughter. It may sound strange. But there was as much happiness in me in that simple little moment as when I walked up the gangway of a Holland America cruise ship a few years ago at the start of a Caribbean cruise with JoAnn.

Perhaps the expectations we load on to "big" events work against us sometimes. Reality has a difficult time living up to them.

In any event, I find more and more that gold – the gold of joy, happiness and love – is in the little everyday moments of life. It's "hiding in plain sight." All it needs is our attention.

Chapter 21

Just Sit Quietly
and See What Happens

"The soul always knows what to do to heal itself. The challenge is to silence the mind."
– Caroline Myss

"All of man's difficulties are caused by his inability to sit quietly in a room."
– Blaise Pascal

Here's a true story that happened recently. I like to do the right thing on Sunday and make breakfast for JoAnn and myself. Mind you, I only really have one culinary skill – but it's a good one, handed down through many generations of British ancestors.

I'm very good at boiling eggs. So as usual yesterday, JoAnn and I each had a boiled egg and toast – the eggs boiled, though I say so myself, to perfection. Nothing unusual so far, right? We ate our breakfast, and I put everything away properly like a good husband should.

I had planned to go for a nice walk after breakfast, but after finishing up in the kitchen a strong compulsion arose in me just to sit down in my favorite chair and be still.

I try to follow my inner "nudges," so I put the walk aside and sat down obediently in my chair. Immediately, a thought came up, "You could read the newspaper." But reading the paper didn't feel right.

With no previous intention on my part I disappeared, as it were, into a "thought-free zone." For about an hour, I simply sat in my chair, utterly surrendered to an experience of happiness and joy that in one sense felt very new and in another sense familiar.

It was like being bathed by love. Once in a while a thought came up, but I just wasn't interested. The joy and peace that I was experiencing was so beautiful, complete, and compelling.

We tend to be afraid of stillness. Being busy is what keeps us sane, or so we think. But remarkable things happen when we give ourselves permission to sit quietly. Many years ago my wife, an intuitive lady, was sitting in her favorite chair in her small townhome in Denver wondering, "Is this all I'm supposed be doing with my life?"

Suddenly she had a momentary sense that someone was sitting in the empty chair across the room. It was such an extraordinary experience that it disoriented her for a few moments. Then, almost immediately, the phone started to ring. It was me, in Vancouver, also feeling a bit stuck, wondering what my next move in life was supposed to be.

I had never met JoAnn, but I knew who she was because we had belonged to the same spiritual group for many years. I decided to give her a call because I planned to visit Colorado to attend a retreat, and the thought arose, "Why not call JoAnn and see if we can have a coffee together?" That's how we got together. We married a year later.

Listen to Pascal's wise words. Give yourself permission to sit quietly in your chair for a few moments and see what happens. You may be amazed.

Chapter 22

Trust Your Own Indomitable Spirit

"It is inevitable that some defeat will enter even the most victorious life. The human spirit is never finished when it is defeated... it is finished when it surrenders."

– Ben Stein

"We run, not because we think it is doing us good, but because we enjoy it and cannot help ourselves. The more restricted our society and work become, the more necessary it will be to find some outlet for this craving for freedom. No one can say, 'You must not run faster than this, or jump higher than that.' The human spirit is indomitable."

– Roger Bannister

The last time I saw my Dad was when he saw me off at the train station at Eastbourne, a seaside town on the south coast of England. We said goodbye at the ticket barrier, but as I walked toward the train a voice inside me said, "Turn around and watch your father." I'm so glad I listened to that voice.

Dad was 94. He lived alone in a small ground-floor flat directly across from his favorite pub in a village called Pevensey Bay, not far from Eastbourne. I had come over from British Columbia to visit him. He died less than a year later at the age of 95.

As I stood at the barrier and watched Dad walk slowly and deliberately toward the exit, I marveled at how upright he was, and I felt a quickening of love and admiration for him I had never felt before in my whole life.

He was 6'3". He was careful, and yet so unutterably proud, in the way he walked. Erect. Straight as a ramrod. Careful, though, not to take too big of a step. Careful in the way he used his stick to help him. Careful not to trip or fall, and all the time never losing his poise.

Left to Right: my Aunt Kathleen, my wonderful wife JoAnn, and Dad

What I saw bursting through him with each step he took was his indomitable spirit. A spirit tried in peace and war. In 75 years of brave journalism – to quote a commemorative silver plate he received toward the end of his life from fellow London journalists – and in a million other ways.

He was as brave at 94 as he was when in his sixties he listened to a judge sentence him to 6 months in prison for refusing to disclose his sources to a government spy tribunal.

His quick jokes, a specialty of his, didn't diminish in quality as far as I could see, and he remained as gallant as ever to the ladies. It impressed the heck out of my wife the first time they met when he insisted on carrying her coat.

It sometimes seems as if there is less and less upon which we can depend these days. But there is one thing you can always trust, and that is your own victorious spirit. It will never let you down no matter what challenges life may bring. Ben Stein speaks the truth when he says the human spirit is never finished when it is defeated, but it is finished when it surrenders.

Chapter 23

100 Steps to Joy

"There are random moments – tossing a salad, coming up the driveway to the house, ironing the seams flat on a quilt square, standing at the kitchen window and looking out at the delphiniums, hearing a burst of laughter from one of my children's rooms – when I feel a wavelike rush of joy. This is my true religion: arbitrary moments of nearly painful happiness for a life I feel privileged to lead."

– Elizabeth Berg

"Love is a force more formidable than any other. It is invisible – it cannot be seen or measured, yet it is powerful enough to transform you in a moment, and offer you more joy than any material possession could."

– Barbara de Angelis

I wrote these thoughts down in a "flow of consciousness" one day. I hope they will give you some new ideas about how to create joy in your life.

1. Pick up a stone and admire it.

2. After you put the stone down look at your hand and admire that. Have you ever seen a more beautiful creation?

3. Put a hand on your belly and do some abdominal breathing, with only your belly moving.

4. My dad, who was in great shape until he died at 95, used to make a point of thinking of something pleasant before he went to sleep. Try it, and see if it works for you.

5. Read the 23rd Psalm.

6. Read a verse or two from *Gitanjali, Love Songs to the Creator*, by Rabindranath Tagore, the revered poet of India. It has certainly blessed my life.

7. Does life seem so transitory sometimes? Consider the possibility that at the core of your being you are timeless and changeless.

8. Look at a photo of your mother and honor her.

9. Don't look to the world for a sense of importance – look within, to your own being.

10. Look up at the sky.

11. Consider the timeless words: "My yoke is easy, my burden is light."

12. Be still.

13. Be still some more.

14. Listen to your own inner voice and trust it.

15. Say "thank you" and really mean it.

16. Consider the possibility that you don't have to look for happiness because who you truly are is already happy.

17. Do the thing your mind says it doesn't want to do.

18. Trust life.

19. Don't let thoughts dictate your life.

20. Why see thoughts as an enemy? Notice that thoughts come and go but the truth of you is always here.

21. Listen to the sweet sound of running water.

22. Be of equal grace to all.

23. Thank your spouse or partner for the many gifts they bring to your life.

24. Trust that life is good and if you play your part everything will unfold as it should.

25. Find some ducks somewhere and admire them.

26. Remember it's never too late to change your mind.

27. Remember it's never too late to be happy.

28. Don't keep your happiness to yourself. Spread it around.

29. Wondering what to do as you age? Consider starting a blog. Remember, it's never too late to be a blogger.

30. Don't close up when strong feelings come. I tried it for a long, long time, and it doesn't work. Let yourself feel your feelings no matter how painful they may be.

31. Discover paradox. Accept paradox. Realize that true nature is strong and also gentle.

32. It's never too late to get in shape. Consider going to a gym. You may find it's a lifesaver.

33. Spend more time with Nature.

34. Admire the beauty of the sky and remind yourself that it simply reflects your own beauty.

35. The sky reflects back to us the spaciousness of our true nature, just as a deer or flower or robin reminds us of the oneness of creation.

36. Never pass up an opportunity to pat a dog – unless, of course, you suspect it might be best left alone.

37. If someone has helped you, or done their best to help you, make sure they know how much you appreciate them.

38. If you are in despair remember that on the other side of despair is joy.

39. It's the joy of our own true nature, untouched and unchanged by any of the adversities of life.

40. We come into this world with a unique gift to give. It's the gift of our own presence.

41. Take time to listen to the sounds around you, your own breathing, the clock on the wall, some passing geese, or the laughter of a child.

42. Don't only listen to external sounds. Listen also to the wisdom of your own spirit speaking to you in the quietness of your heart.

43. Be brave.

44. Be patient. Patience is one of the greatest gifts of the universe. As long as you are doing the best you know how in this moment, don't be concerned about the future. It will take care of itself.

45. Take pleasure in little things.

46. Take pleasure in the chickadee and her unique little cries.

47. Take pleasure in the sight of a woman enjoying her children or grandchildren.

48. Give thanks for the gift your own physical body has given you.

49. Is your body getting old, or having troubles at the moment? Acknowledge how faithful it has been through the years.

50. Don't be afraid if you lose something precious. There is one thing you can never lose – your own boundless nature.

51. Do something silly. Whatever your age, come out to play.

52. Sing the next time you vacuum the house.

53. Just because you have done something a certain way before doesn't mean you have to keep doing it the same way.

54. Life is a victorious experience when we live it with a victorious spirit.

55. There are riches and joys waiting to be revealed that we have never even dreamed of yet.

56. Persistence is part of your true nature. There is always more persistence available to us.

57. Life is a trickster though. There are times when persistence is NOT called for.

58. Remember Khalil Gibran's wise words, "Who bakes bread without love bakes a bitter bread that feeds but half man's hunger."

59. When in doubt, smile.

60. Do some more abdominal breathing right now.

61. It's good to be whole. The truth is you are already whole.

62. Ever think about looking into Chi Gung? It has many gifts to give, especially as we age.

63. A wonderful resource on Chi Gung is *The Way of Energy* by Master Lam Kam Chuen.

64. Be kind to yourself.

65. These are some words I like to say to myself sometimes when I am in trouble: "Everything is going to be all right."

66. Maybe the words have their power because my mother said them to me in the early days of WWII as bombs fell all around our apartment block in central London.

67. Never forget the sea, and its wonderful healing energy.

68. Just listening to the roar and rumble of the sea will uplift the lowliest spirit.

69. The sea is primeval like the lion and the forest, and you and me.

70. Stop and listen to the hum of the universe in your ear.

71. Stop and note the magnificence of the universe in a fine painting, or in a mountain, or in a brightly colored butterfly.

72. Be true to yourself. Honor yourself. Above all, listen to the voice of your own being in the quietness of your heart.

73. Feel the skin of your left hand. Isn't it a miracle?

74. Pick a blade of grass this summer and stick it between your teeth like you did when you were young.

75. My favorite picture hangs above my computer. It shows a young fox at rest on a mound of earth with a piece of grass in his teeth, eyes shut and face aglow with bliss.

76. Bliss is our true nature. Don't let go of your bliss, follow it wherever it takes you.

77. Don't be too quick to form an opinion of someone – it takes time to really get to know another person.

78. Reach out and try something new.

79. Who are you, really? Suppose you are an aspect of Eternal Love finding expression through human form. Our forms come and go – but the love that you truly are has neither beginning nor end.

80. "Love never fails." Were more beautiful words ever written?

81. Where are the limits of love? Does it have any limits?

82. Love is not bound by time. I just thought of my mother, long gone, and felt a closeness with her that is as strong now as it ever was.

83. If love transcends time, perhaps it also transcends space?

84. If the truth of your being is love, and you get on a plane and go somewhere, do you really go anywhere?

85. Perhaps, when we think we travel, or move from here to there, we are fooling ourselves.

86. Perhaps the truth of you has not moved at all.

87. Perhaps here is the secret of true peace.

88. I've got to say a word in support of ravens. I love ravens. I'm so glad that the townhome complex where JoAnn and I live has a resident flock of ravens we can listen to and watch every day.

89. Don't only look for happiness in big things like a relationship, or a trip to Hawaii or Bali. Look for joy in little moments like going for a walk, drinking a cup of tea, or chatting with a friend.

90. Bliss is a gift from the universe. It's who we are. It's part of our divine nature.

91. Let the joy that is already inside you express through you to bless your life and the lives of others.

92. Joy is our true name. It was our name before we came into this world, and it will still be our name when we say goodbye to our earthly body that has been our home and friend in this life.

93. The more responsibility you take for your own life the happier you will be.

94. The more responsibility we take for our planet the happier it will be.

95. Joy and freedom. Freedom and joy. Such beautiful words, aren't they?

96. I'm writing this in a suburb of Denver in sunny Colorado. Wherever you are, and wherever you live, I send best wishes to you.

97. We are not as separate from one another as we may think.

98. You are part of a beautiful, intelligent whole.

99. You are loved by this whole.

100. Trust your own unconquerable spirit.

Chapter 24

Top 10 Ways to Be Unhappy

"Don't wait around for other people to be happy for you. Any happiness you get you've got to make yourself."

— Alice Walker

"The unhappy person resents it when you try to cheer him up, because that means he has to stop dwelling on himself and start paying attention to the universe. Unhappiness is the ultimate form of self-indulgence. When you're unhappy, you get to pay a lot of attention to yourself. You get to take yourself oh so very seriously."

— Tom Robbins

I've got a brilliant idea. Obviously, most of us want to be happy and joyful. But a few people actually enjoy being miserable. This is a small minority, I'm sure. But although there are lots of books that help people to become happier, who is there standing up for people who enjoy being unhappy?

Where are the self-help books that help them?

It seems only fair to me, therefore, to include a few simple tips in this book to help people who like being miserable become even more miserable. I would like to add that I have personally tested each of these steps.

1. Never be still.

    Never, ever be still. Keep yourself busy and distracted at all times. You have to realize that stillness is your number one enemy, because if you give it half a chance it will open a door to undreamed-of joy and bliss. I don't care if this is a conscious realization or an unconscious one – just as long as you refuse to be still under any circumstance.

    My advice? Do whatever it takes. Go on a trip. Buy a new scarf. Get a new car. Get a new husband or wife. Get rid of your present husband or wife. And so on and so forth.

2. Never question your beliefs.

    Never, NEVER question any of your beliefs or prejudices. This can be very dangerous, because it may open your mind to a new sense of the limitless beauty and potential of life. In fact, the more I think about this step, the more I realize that it is just as important as the first step. In any case, just realize that if you dare to question any of your beliefs in this time of rapid change and transformation it may have creative consequences – the very result you are trying to avoid.

3. Stay away from dogs.

Be very careful to have no contact whatsoever with animals, particularly dogs. This is a big mistake that many misery lovers frequently make. Dogs, you see – and many other animals, not to mention birds and trees and whatnot – can make us happy without saying a word. I'm just warning you in the strongest possible terms – stay away from dogs.

4. Watch out for babies.

The above applies to babies. It's true that babies can sometimes make us irritated or angry. But it's a well-known fact that a baby can change our mood for the better in an instant – even more effectively than dogs can. Babies are a special problem that deserves more attention than I can give in this brief guide.

5. Repeat this mantra every day.

At the beginning of every day, repeat this mantra three times. It's most effective when spoken aloud, but if circumstances prevent that, just repeat the words in your head. Say to yourself with as much conviction as possible:

"This is going to be a terrible day. I just know it's going to be an awful day."

6. Congratulate yourself on your misery.

    At the end of the day, don't forget to take a moment to look back and congratulate yourself. Think how much misery you were able to create for yourself using these simple techniques.

7. Distract yourself from the present moment.

    This is another key step in the program. Distract yourself as much as possible from the present moment. TV is an effective tool in this regard. So is complaining about the weather. I guarantee that the more you can train yourself to do this the more miserable you will be.

8. Remember you are better than most people.

    Make it a guiding principle to remember that you are a little bit better than most people you meet. One or two exceptions are okay. But remind yourself of this every day.
    Supermarkets are a good place to practice. Subways are equally good.
    This is a wonderful way to isolate yourself and preserve that gnawing sense of emptiness and loneliness that we are seeking to preserve.

9. Be careful what books you read.

Be very careful what books you read. Read only books that support your views. By the same token, carefully censor which TV talk-show hosts you watch, which radio stations you listen to, and so on.

10. Finally, if you really want to remain enmeshed in a bottomless pit of despair, and achieve the best results with this unique self-help program, never allow that ridiculous notion called "Hope" to take root in your heart. It can be very dangerous.

I do hope these tips are helpful. I wish you the best of luck and would be pleased to receive any feedback from you. If you have any other helpful ideas you'd like to share, please do send them to me.

Chapter 25

It's Never Too Late to Be a Handyman

"Vulnerability is the only authentic state. Being vulnerable means being open, for wounding, but also for pleasure. Being open to the wounds of life means also being open to the bounty and beauty. Don't mask or deny your vulnerability: it is your greatest asset."
                                                    – Stephen Russell

"Life is a song – sing it. Life is a game – play it. Life is a challenge – meet it. Life is a dream – realize it. Life is a sacrifice – offer it. Life is love – enjoy it."
                                                    – Sai Baba

It's never too late to be a handyman, I learned the other day. My dad was a great journalist, but went through his entire life hardly knowing what a screwdriver was. It was like he prided himself on not being very good with tools – and I grew up with the same approach.

So here's what happened. I had just finished watering the bushes in the front of our townhome when JoAnn asked me to hose down the front door and windows. Which I did. About 30 minutes later, as we were having lunch, the front doorbell rang. "Who can that be?" we wondered. I went to the front door, but there was nobody there.

After lunch it was time for our afternoon rest, a wonderful survival strategy for people of a certain age. We had just got comfortable when the doorbell rang again. So of course I got up to answer – but once again, to my surprise, there was no one there.

To cut a long story short, the front doorbell continued to ring every hour or two – with never a visitor in sight – until finally, around five o'clock, I realized I had to do something about the situation. "We don't want to be listening to the front doorbell all night, do we?" I asked JoAnn.

Presumably spraying water all over the doorbell had made it angry. But while the urgency of our situation was beginning to dawn on me, the problem was, what was I going to do about it? My first thought was, naturally, to call someone for help. But it was Memorial Day. I couldn't call an electrician or a professional handyman on a holiday like that, could I?

I summoned my British spirit and took a bold step. "It won't hurt to take the cover off the doorbell panel in the hallway and have a look at it," I said to JoAnn.

I got something to stand on, removed the cover and inspected the mechanism. I saw it included two wires, each fastened down on separate little plates by a screw.

Here is where I am quite proud of myself. It occurred to me that these wires obviously played an important part in making the whole thing work. And if I could somehow detach them, the doorbell that was threatening our peace of mind and would definitely sabotage our sleep might have a hard time ringing, right?

I went and grabbed a screwdriver from my toolbox. Yes, I do have a toolbox. It isn't very big, about a foot long by 6 inches wide, but there are a few things in it that can be useful, like some string, a pair of pliers etc.

Just for a moment a thought flitted through my mind, "I wonder if I might get an electric shock?" But I dismissed it and JoAnn was actually very impressed when I loosened the two screws I've told you about and pried the wires loose.

"Don't see how it can work now," I said smugly. And indeed that is how it worked out. In fact the doorbell is still blissfully quiet as I write about this incident. Dad would be proud of me, I'm sure. Perhaps there's a handyman in all of us just waiting to step forward and go to work?

Chapter 26

The Joy of Synchronicity

"According to Vedanta, there are only two symptoms of enlightenment, just two indications that a transformation is taking place within you toward a higher consciousness. The first symptom is that you stop worrying. Things don't bother you anymore. You become light-hearted and full of joy. The second symptom is that you encounter more and more meaningful coincidences in your life, more and more synchronicities."

– Deepak Chopra

"I am open to the guidance of synchronicity, and do not let expectations hinder my path."

– The Dalai Lama

One of the joys of aging for me is becoming more conscious of the mysterious process Carl Jung called synchronicity.

One day I received a letter from the principal of a private school in Loveland, Colorado, inviting me to speak to her students about an animal fable I wrote some years ago entitled *The Raven Who Spoke with God.*

It's strange how sometimes our mind likes to come up with objections to something when it often simply doesn't know what should or shouldn't happen. "It's a nice invitation," I thought to myself, "but it's a long trip from Denver. The visit would probably take the whole day. I'm not sure it would be worth it just to speak to a few schoolchildren."

Fortunately, I realized it really was a very special gesture on the part of the principal, and I really did need to go.

My goodness. How glad I am that I accepted the invitation. It proved to be one of the most rewarding and magical experiences of my life.

My story about a brave young raven's heroic mission to restore the honor of his kind was quite successful when it was published. It was picked up by a Spanish publisher named Ediciones B and later translated into 10 other foreign language editions. But it had become clear the book had run its course, and since we planned to move to Denver, I gave away most of my remaining copies to Loveland's Habitat for Humanity before we moved.

Here is where this amazing power of synchronicity clicked in.

Although I thought my book had reached the end of its natural life span, little did I know that life had other ideas for *The Raven Who Spoke with God*.

Beth, the principal of the school (which I believe is closed now, unfortunately), saw a box of the books for sale for a few dollars at a Habitat store and decided to buy them. She was so touched by the story of a young raven who followed his dream despite major challenges that she made the book part of her school curriculum.

When I arrived at the school I had the immense pleasure of meeting a group of students aged about 10 to 16 who loved the book and had been inspired by it to think more deeply about their lives.

Each of the students wrote me a note of appreciation.

Said one: "This book was very inspirational to me in some things that I was going through. I enjoyed having a character like Joshua, who goes through a very hard time at the beginning, but it got better along the way. I'm really happy that you wrote this book, because it showed me that even in the hardest of times God is always there to help you get through it."

Synchronicity is another word for grace, as far as I'm concerned. I will never forget the magical day I spent meeting Beth and her students.

I had always hoped my raven book would help people overcome their challenges and achieve their goals and aspirations. But suppose Beth had not bought the box of books I gave away to Habitat? Or suppose she had left the book unread? Then what? I would never have met some wonderful young people whose passion for truth will inspire me as long as I live.

Don't be too quick to give up on your dreams. Synchronicity may touch your life at any time and in ways you perhaps could never imagine.

Chapter 27

The Wonder of a Child's Gaze

"The further I wake into this life, the more I realize that God is everywhere and the extraordinary is waiting quietly beneath the skin of all that is ordinary. Light is in both the broken bottle and the diamond, and music is in both the flowing violin and the water dripping from the drainage pipe. Yes, God is under the porch as well as on top of the mountain, and joy is in both the front row and the bleachers, if we are willing to be where we are."

– Mark Nepo

"Be aware of wonder. Live a balanced life – learn some and think some and draw and paint and sing and dance and play and work every day some."

– Robert Fulghum

One day a neighbor came over to visit JoAnn and me with her little boy, Maxwell, who was then 16 months old.

After cruising around the house, checking things out like the good little supervisor he is,

Maxwell decided it was time to check me out. He came over and stood beside me, looking at me intently, and I had a sudden notion to pick him up and hold him in my lap.

His mom smiled and nodded her approval, so I picked up this quiet, very curious, strong faced little child and sat him on my lap. He sat there for the longest time, absolutely still, simply looking at me. It's difficult to describe the innocence, wonder and primeval wisdom I saw in his eyes as I returned his gaze. It was like looking into the eyes of the universe. JoAnn told me later that Maxwell had a look of complete bliss on his face.

"He never does that," said his mom, amazed. "He never sits quietly like that."

Finally Maxwell, who had a chocolate chip cookie in his hand, held it out to me so I could have a bite too. I pretended to nibble away at it like a mouse, which brought a big grin to his face. Then he went even further, offering me his sippy cup.

A magical encounter indeed, and yet so simple and ordinary. The opportunity to be consciously present in life's little moments is surely one of the greatest treasures of aging.

Chapter 28

You Are Loved

"I believe that you're great, that there's something magnificent about you. Regardless of what has happened to you in your life, regardless of how young or how old you think you might be, the moment you begin to think properly, there's something that is within you, there's power within you, that's greater than the world."

       – Michael Bernard Beckwith

"Love is like the wind, you can't see it but you can feel it."

       – Nicholas Sparks

Be joyful. Be happy. You are magnificent, just as Dr. Beckwith says. You are a masterpiece. You are an essential part of this universe and you are loved.

  We are all loved without exception because we reside in a universe built by love and operated by love. Young or old, rich or poor, whatever your circumstances or your nationality, and regardless of whether you are religious or not – you are loved.

Regardless of your foibles, you are loved. I say this with some confidence because none of my own foibles has succeeded in changing the love that lives within me and emanates each day from the depths of my being.

Love was with us when we were born and it will be with us when we die.

Yes, it's true that romantic love tends to come and go. But we are talking now of a power beyond our human imagining that is boundless and forever free. It does not come and go. Its love includes every cell of our body, and though we may never fully understand it, we can experience its presence each moment of our lives.

There I was, not so many years ago, feeling utterly alone, confused, and lost as I contemplated the abrupt loss of my wife and the collapse of the community to which I had given my life for 36 years.

Did the love of which I am speaking abandon me? No, it did not. I felt like I was being run through a wringer, mind you. I knew despair more intense than anything I have ever known. But the grace that abides in each of us knew of my plight.

The universe was aware of what was going on in my life as it is aware of what is transpiring in your life. And though I thought I was lost, I wasn't, really. Step by step the universe, in its grace, took me by the hand and showed me a path to a new life. It opened the door to a new experience of freedom and joy that I could never have imagined in my wildest dreams.

Do you face difficult times right now? Is despair knocking at your door? I have learned the same lesson that Dr. Beckwith has learned. There is something magnificent in us that can never be defeated.

All we have to do is be true to ourselves and keep expressing the love that is in us to the best of our ability. As we do this, walls will disappear before us and we will discover with great joy that it doesn't really matter what life throws at us.

Your true nature is untouched by any of your adversities and it is not going to be defeated.

Chapter 29

Some Things We Can Learn from Nature

"Look deep into nature, and then you will understand everything better."

– Albert Einstein

"Forget not that the earth delights to feel your bare feet and the winds long to play with your hair."

– Khalil Gibran

Our wild bunny came home late yesterday. He – or is it she? – lives under the big blue spruce tree outside our front door and likes to take off every now and again, so that sometimes we don't see him for three weeks or more at a time.

JoAnn likes to think he is busy visiting various girlfriends in the area, which may be true, of course.

I get a bit concerned as weeks go by with no bunny in sight. I wonder if mischief of some kind has befallen him. His life is fragile, just like ours, with coyotes and other threats present in the region.

Bunny, as far as I know, does not have the ability or the wish to kill or maim anything or anyone. He survives, if he does survive, because he can run as fast as a speeding locomotive and has a highly honed early warning system.

He survives, too, because he is a creature of the earth. He finds protection, comfort and renewal in the embrace of mother earth and in the deep, winding tunnels that he (or is it she?) builds below ground. Gosh, I wonder who does do most of the work, come to think of it?

I feel a deep connection with this simple but magical creature. Perhaps one reason is that although bunnies are obviously insignificant as far as human affairs are concerned – though they can be a nuisance, of course – they actually have a lot to teach us.

For instance:

1. Bunny reminds me to examine my own tools of perception and how well I use them. I may not have the radar-like hearing or almost 360-degree vision of a rabbit, but I have other perceptive abilities.

   For example, do I listen to the nudges of my heart? Do I pay attention to the spirit behind another person's utterance? Do I trust my instincts if I feel a need to be cautious in some situation?

2. Bunny reminds me of the value of play. He and his fellow rabbits like to hop and jump for no apparent reason. I have read that they can jump as high as nine feet. One time JoAnn and I looked out the window of our previous home and saw a bunny running around in small circles in our backyard, sometimes stopping to throw a little jump into the mix. Why was that? Well, as far as I'm concerned, it was purely for the fun of it.

   How I thank God that over the past few years particularly, I have remembered this innate ability we all have to be playful. The older I become the more I enjoy not taking myself so seriously and being playful just for the sake of being playful. The more I enjoy seeing the fun present in little moments.

3. Bunny reminds me to stay "grounded." It is good to let thoughts and imagination roam. It is wonderful to dream, and dream big. But bunny reminds me that just as he finds renewal and sanctuary in his burrow, so I must find well-being in life's simple tasks and in simple moments like playing with a child or admiring a tree or listening to the music of the stream that flows behind our property.

4. Last but not least, our resident bunny reminds me of the importance of vulnerability. We have been conditioned to think that to be strong means we must always be right, and never wrong. We have been told it's weak to change our mind or see another person's point of view.

   But there is no real strength without vulnerability. How thankful we may be that strength and compassion walk together hand in hand. We have the privilege of exhibiting both these virtues in a balanced manner in our lives. Our happiness and the happiness of others depend upon it.

Part Three

Inner Peace

Chapter 30

Be Thankful For Your Body

"The higher your energy level, the more efficient your body. The more efficient your body, the better you feel and the more you will use your talent to produce outstanding results."

– Tony Robbins

"I made a commitment to completely cut out drinking and anything that might hamper me from getting my mind and body together. And the floodgates of goodness have opened upon me – spiritually and financially."

– Denzel Washington

I can't help but be aware, as years go by, of the changes transpiring in this physical body that has been my home for more than 80 years. Goodness, is it my imagination? The font that I like to use to compose my posts looks a bit smaller to me today than usual. That can't really be the case, can it?

How loyal this body of mine has been. How brave it has been. Many hardships and challenges have been visited upon this lean but wiry body since it was first created, and it has withstood them all.

I have a scar about 3 inches long and half an inch wide on the inside of my leg. When I was 6 years old, I went for a walk in the woods with my parents and got caught while trying to climb over a barbed wire fence. I can only imagine how loudly I cried and the concern my parents felt. But my body didn't complain in the least. It just went calmly to work to heal the big gash I had received.

My body – like yours – has experienced much tribulation. But it is still here. It is still doing its very best to handle the challenges that life brings and maintain a balance in these difficult times.

The time does come, of course, when our bodies can no longer continue to serve us. A good friend named Martin, who is 86, was recently moved to a hospice. He and his wife are neighbors of ours. I visited him a few days back and it was such a pleasure to be with him and chat about this and that, about the gigantic Tom Clancy thriller on his bedside table, about the great food he is getting, about the pretty fountain and birds outside his window.

I don't know exactly when Martin will pass from this human scene, but I know he will pass with serenity and grace because that is how he has lived his life. I think he sees death as just another circumstance to handle.

Perhaps it's a bit like getting ready to go on a trip. I sense that Martin and his wife, married for 65 years, have done what they need to do to prepare for the journey and can face the future with equanimity because there are no unresolved issues hanging over their heads.

What a paradox life is. Yes, my friend's body is coming to the end of its natural life – just as my own body will come to the end of its natural life. But while our bodies are obviously finite, the serenity and grace that I experience when I am in Martin's presence is not finite. It is Love, and it is eternal. It is Love, and it is the base of wholeness, well-being and peace.

Let us be thankful for our bodies. Surely, they are our best friend, doing their best whatever comes.

Chapter 31

Can Animals Sense Goodness In Us?

"A dog has no use for fancy cars, big homes, or designer clothes. A water-logged stick will do just fine. A dog doesn't care if you're rich or poor, clever or dull, smart or dumb. Give him your heart and he'll give you his. How many people can you say that about? How many people can make you feel rare and pure and special?"

– John Grogan

"I ask people why they have deer heads on their walls. They always say because it's such a beautiful animal. There you go. I think my mother is attractive, but I have photographs of her."

– Ellen DeGeneres

I received a touching email from a reader of my blog, in which he asked me the following question:

"Do you think animals and young children can sense goodness in you? Almost everywhere I go animals gravitate toward me and babies smile at me and make eye contact like they know me. I don't really understand it, and often think it's because I look like I'm not a threat to animals or I'm funny looking to children. My wife says it's because I'm a kindred spirit and they recognize it in me. The way I was brought up taught me otherwise. I'm not special, and no matter what I do it will never be good enough."

I absolutely think that animals and young children can sense goodness in us. I was reading an interesting article in *The Telegraph* that reported how a team from Florida University carried out two experiments involving domesticated dogs and their relative, the wolf.

The two sets of animals were given an opportunity to beg for food – either from an attentive, compassionate person or from a person who wasn't interested in helping a potential beggar. Both the wolves and the domestic dogs approached those people who, as the article put it, were "attentive."

Some people (and you are surely one of these) do seem to have a special gift when it comes to relating to animals. For example, if there is a dog in a room and my wife sits down in that room, I guarantee the dog will come over and plant itself by my wife's feet. Then it will just sit there, as if glued in place, staring blissfully at nothing too much.

JoAnn doesn't do anything to encourage this sort of canine behavior. I think she'd be quite happy if dogs ignored her. But they don't ignore her – just as they don't ignore you, apparently.

I'm sure your wife is absolutely right. Animals gravitate toward you and babies smile at you because they sense you are a loving person who just naturally appreciates them.

I'm sorry your upbringing instilled the notion that you are not all that remarkable and nothing you do will ever be good enough. Many of us have been tarred by that brush. But I have some good news for you. Nothing that has been done to you in life has actually harmed the essential "you." You have a unique gift to give and this gift, whatever it is, is unhurt by any of the conditioning of your life to this point.

All you have to do and all you can do is to continue giving your gift as best you know how and everything will work out just fine. Dr. Phil made a good point in an article my wife was reading yesterday, "There has to be something in your life that makes you want to hop out of bed and kick butt. It can be your job, spiritual life, family, sports – anything that invigorates you."

What brings you joy? Look deep. The answer is there. Perhaps you will find your passion working with animals? Whatever your gift is, trust life and your heart will show you the way.

Chapter 32

How a Wooden Sword Gave Me Strength

"Words of kindness are more healing to a drooping heart than balm or honey."

– Sarah Fielding

"For me, singing sad songs often has a way of healing a situation. It gets the hurt out in the open into the light, out of the darkness."

– Reba McEntire

A wooden sword sits on a window ledge in my little office. It's a replica of a Chinese sword from the age of the samurai and it has quite a story to tell.

Once upon a time, as I've mentioned earlier in this book, there were three constants in my life. At least, I thought they were constants. It would never have entered my head that one day one of these constants might cease to exist – let alone that all three might disappear within a few short years.

But they did vanish. I lost my spiritual mentor who I had loved and followed for more than 35 years. I lost my wife, Joy. And finally, on a cold morning in October 1994, I said goodbye forever to the spiritual community that had been my home for so long in British Columbia.

This is where my wooden sword comes into the picture. Of course, it wasn't the sword itself that helped me heal. It was what it symbolized to me.

My entire world had shattered. I was in a state of numbness, denial, and terrible grief. I felt I was on the edge of an abyss, with virtually no money and no prospects that I could see – what was I going to do?

Thank God, the first step was clear enough. It was to go to Vancouver, 300 miles to the south, where my son Durwin lived. I will always be so thankful for the friendship and support he offered to me, and offers to this day.

A day or two after arriving in Vancouver to begin what seemed the hopeless task of rebuilding my life, I had a sudden impulse. "Go to Chinatown and buy a wooden sword," said my inner voice. "It will be a symbol of the warrior spirit that you will need to handle this situation you're in."

I remember so well taking a bus to Chinatown and then, because this was Vancouver, getting soaked as I walked for several blocks in heavy rain looking for a suitable sword. Finally I found one, and in the difficult, confusing days that followed, this wooden sword did indeed help me navigate the challenge before me.

Perhaps a physical symbol of some kind has been a blessing in your life, or is a blessing right now. JoAnn was telling me the other day how for many years she was troubled by the notion that her mother loved her sister more than she loved her.

One day JoAnn was looking at a portrait of herself taken when she was about 8 years old when she realized that this idea she had carried with her for so long simply wasn't true. She recognized how happy she looked, and how nicely dressed she was – with cute Shirley Temple curls her mother had put in her hair. She realized her mother really did love her and a lifetime burden lifted in her.

Change is inevitable. Tragedy and loss can strike at any time. But as we persevere and "keep the faith," to quote a wise therapist I once knew, a path to healing will emerge.

Chapter 33

The Healing Power of Ritual

"Ritual isn't about doing a routine mindlessly. It's a way of building something good into your life, so that you don't forget what's important."

– Leo Babauta

"My only ritual is to just sit down and write, write every day."

– Augusten Burroughs

A ritual has been defined as "a set of actions which often have symbolic value." I like to think of ritual the same way Leo Babauta does, as a routine that in a simple but practical way gives us courage and comfort, helping us to meet the challenges of life more effectively.

In my early 20s, I ran into a difficult time when I returned home to London to "settle down" after spending some time in Southern Rhodesia (now Zimbabwe) and New Zealand. I felt confused and alienated from my British middle class background, even as an inner voice proclaimed loudly and fiercely that there was a true purpose for my life and I needed to get busy and find it.

The day before leaving Auckland to sail home to England I had bought a book called *Leaves of Grass*, by Walt Whitman. I had never heard of the great poet but the book seemed to call to me as I prowled a bookshop looking for something to read on the voyage home.

The book was my constant companion for two years. I read a little bit of Whitman every day. The book was with me when I went to work as a reporter on the *Daily Express* newspaper in London. It was with me when I went sailing in my small boat on the Essex coast. It was still with me when at the age of 23 I went to western Canada to find a new life.

Then one day I didn't feel the need to read Walt Whitman any more. My "ritual" came to an end as naturally and spontaneously as it had begun. I still loved Walt but I didn't need his help any longer.

Here are a few rituals that bring joy to my life:

1. Abdominal breathing first thing in the morning and last thing at night helps bring calm and focus.

2. Working out at the gym makes me feel strong.

3. Telling JoAnn how wonderful she is makes me feel good.

4. Going to the coffee shop in the afternoon gets me away from my little office and gives me a chance to read and connect with other people, or perhaps not do anything at all.

5. Appreciating little moments opens my mind and heart to life's magic.

6. A glass of wine on the porch in the evening lets me commune with Nature and passers-by – and perhaps pat their dogs.

7. Listening to birds soothes my soul.

8. Watching the evening news connects me with the world.

Rituals give structure to our lives. They give us a track to run on. But it's important to be flexible – not afraid to create new routines, particularly when they arise spontaneously in our lives, and not afraid to let them go either when they have served their purpose.

Chapter 34

9 Steps to a New Life

"Today expect something good to happen to you no matter what occurred yesterday. Realize the past no longer holds you captive. It can only continue to hurt you if you hold on to it. Let the past go. A simply abundant world awaits."

– Sarah Ban Breathnach

"Throughout life people will make you mad, disrespect you and treat you bad. Let God deal with the things they do, cause hate in your heart will consume you too."

– Will Smith

One day a reader of my blog sent me a message saying he was in the middle of a messy divorce that also affected a number of children.

"I'm having a difficult time dealing with the rejection and being all alone in an empty apartment with my clothes and laptop," he said. "Do you have any advice on how I can let go, rebuild and move on to a meaningful life?"

Here are some suggestions I made to this man. Mind you, I'm sure I would have included Sarah Ban Breathnach's advice at the top of this page if I had known about it.

1. Let yourself feel your feelings.

   This can be a difficult thing to do, especially when our feelings are painful, frightening, and hard to bear. We've been conditioned – at least I was – to try to escape unpleasant feelings. We suppress them. We try to distract ourselves in some way.

   It simply doesn't work. I have found after much trauma that the quickest route to healing and happiness – in fact the only route – is to allow ourselves to feel our feelings at all costs. It opens the door to new growth. New possibilities emerge in our lives. Giving yourself permission to experience your feelings is not "soft" or weak. It has nothing to do with being a victim. It takes real strength to feel what you are feeling without either wallowing in it or trying to escape from it.

2. Create a daily ritual.

   So here's a suggestion. Create a daily ritual or ceremony. It won't be forever, just until you begin to feel some relief and confidence. For example, take 10 minutes a day (whenever you can fit it in – perhaps in the evening) when the only thing you do is sit quietly in a chair and feel whatever comes up in your heart.

You may be surprised by the power of this ritual. It helps you reconnect with yourself at a deeper level. Also, if a painful feeling does come up during the day, you can remind yourself that it's okay – it will have a chance to be heard at your next quiet time.

3. Do whatever comforts you and enlivens you.

One of my lifelines, when I was deep in despair, was continuing to visit my favorite coffee shop each afternoon. The world might be falling apart beneath my feet, but the coffee shop didn't seem to be fazed by my tribulations at all.

The people who served me coffee were as cheerful as ever. And just being aware of other people being "normal" – living "normal" lives as they went about their business, sipping their lattes, telling stories, discussing business, or working hard at their computer – was very therapeutic.

It helped to relieve my sense of isolation and reminded me that no matter what was going on in my own life, I was part of the larger family of humankind and there was a big blessing in that.

4. Do something for someone else.

   This piece of wisdom has been around for a long time, but this is because it works. It connects us immediately with the kindness and compassion at the core of our being.

   And by the way, it doesn't have to be something big or spectacular. Just smiling at a neighbor or a lady serving you in a supermarket will do it. Little steps to serenity and well-being are just as important as big steps – perhaps even more important.

5. Perhaps you can volunteer for a worthwhile cause that is important to you. If you need some ideas or inspiration in this regard, volunteermatch.org might be a good place to start.

6. Stay close to Nature.

   Staying close to Nature helps keep us grounded in times of trouble. Find a stream and listen to it. Look at a tree and admire it. Or how about getting a dog?

   JoAnn and I don't have a dog, but we live in a townhouse complex in which quite a few people do have dogs. I find patting a neighbor's dog is very therapeutic. The dog usually enjoys it too.

7. Let go of your wife.

As long as you are estranged from each other, your wife is the last person you should look to right now for any kind of help or useful conversation. Give her the dignity and space to pursue her own path at this juncture in her life while you do the same.

8. Get regular exercise.

Exercise can be a lifesaver in times of trouble. Research has shown that exercise helps burn up stress hormones – amazing, isn't it?

9. Forgive your ex-wife.

Lastly, please forgive your ex-wife, at all costs. This may be a hard thing to do, especially now. But it's critical both for her sake and also your own.

I send you blessings. I trust these tips may be helpful and wish you all the very best in your ongoing life journey.

Chapter 35

It's Never Too Late to Heal Your Past

"Simply touching a difficult memory with some slight willingness to heal begins to soften the holding and tension around it."

– Stephen Levine

"Every time you are tempted to react in the same old way, ask if you want to be a prisoner of the past or a pioneer of the future."

– Deepak Chopra

Sometimes as we move bravely through our days we carry a burden from our past that ruins the quality of our life now and prevents us from experiencing the blessed life that is our birthright. But suppose we can heal our past if we wish?

Suppose we can see what we imagined was a difficult experience or trauma in our childhood in a new way? For example, I realize now with hindsight that what I thought was a lonely, desolate, wasted period of my life was actually a time of considerable blessing.

I felt alone and abandoned for four long years, from age eight to twelve, when I was evacuated from London to the Devon countryside in the early days of the Blitz. It's true that my aunt Eva was there to take care of me. But the cottage where we lived was quite remote, and I sure felt alone. I had no friends. And with Dad away as a war correspondent in India and Burma, and Mum working in Harrods bookshop in London, I was separated from both of them in what seemed an alien environment.

Before I was evacuated, I'd lived with my mother on the fifth floor of an apartment block in central London. What did I know of the countryside? I was a child of the city. But here's what I see now that I didn't see before.

Being sent to live in a remote cottage at the end of a quiet Devonshire lane – a cottage with no electricity, of course – gave me the opportunity to suddenly become aware of two things that have proved to be critical components of my life ever since.

It opened my eyes to the magic of Nature. And it introduced me to stillness; the primeval stillness that we are conditioned to fear but which I now know is the source of all wisdom, and the door to true meaning and happiness.

What I thought of as wasted years opened my eyes to the magic of birds, fields, and books. I experienced the simple happiness of reading, picking blackberries, and exploring Devon lanes. I was given the gift of safety. I see how miraculous it was when my mother came down to visit from London and we climbed on our bikes and went for long bike rides together to favorite spots on the North Devon coast.

I remember how blissful it was to snuggle in my feather bed while Mum read to me from books that she loved. And I remember the peaceful evenings with my aunt and cousin – after we had lit the Aladdin lamp – playing cards and eating apples that I had picked from the orchard at the rear of the cottage. I am thankful for all of it.

How about your early years? Is there anything you would like to heal, bless, and make whole as you bring it to the light of now, the light of your present day awareness?

Chapter 36

7 Gifts of a Loving Universe

"The truth is true, and all is well. Unconquerable life prevails."

– Lord Martin Cecil

"The truth will not necessarily set you free, but truthfulness will."

– Ken Wilber

You are not as alone or helpless as you may sometimes think. We live in a just and loving universe that has given each of us seven gifts so that we may flourish, endure – and, I'm happy to report, live our dream whatever our age may be. These gifts are as follows:

1. **Patience** makes it possible to not only bear our anguish but also to follow our dream and fulfill our destiny.

2. **Gratitude** opens the door to wisdom. It makes it possible for us to change and to grow. If we have believed a lie, or our attitude to someone

is wrong – we can change. Gratitude opens a door to a new experience of increased meaning and wholeness.

3. **Courage** is the creative power that makes it possible for us to meet the challenges of our lives and give the world our unique gift.

4. **Compassion** sees the pain of the world, but it also sees the beauty and oneness of creation.

5. **Happiness** is a reflection of the joy of the universe in which we live. It is our birthright. It is not something we must struggle hard to find and to hold. All we need to do is to reclaim what is already ours.

6. **Freedom** is given to us so that we may be free to live and love and create in ways that honor the universe of which we are part. Freedom is our true nature. We don't have to change our circumstances to be free. Mind you, we do need to be truthful, as Ken Wilber reminds us in his quote.

7. **Love** bathes us each moment of our lives, whether we realize it consciously or not. As has been said, "The sun shines on the just and the unjust." The universe sees you, admires you, and loves you – because you are part of itself.

The older I become, the more I realize that the order and beauty I see in our universe reflects the same order and beauty that is inherent in us. And the more thankful I become for the mystical oneness that binds all creatures and beings from the furthest star to the tiniest grain of sand. We may never fully understand the universe in which we live but we can certainly appreciate its generosity and wonder.

Chapter 37

The Power of Patience

"You can learn many things from children. How much patience you have, for instance."

— Franklin P. Jones

"A healthy male adult bore consumes each year one and a half times his own weight in other people's patience."

— John Updike

The power of patience is all too easily overlooked in our fast-paced culture. But it's absolutely critical to lasting happiness and inner peace.

True, with more and more people demanding immediate gratification, it might seem patience has become obsolete.

But whatever your age, and whatever your life situation, nurturing this calm and noble quality will yield the same rich rewards today that it always has throughout the entire run of human history.

Of course, it goes without saying that patience can never really be isolated from any of the other qualities of our own true character. "Patience is the companion of wisdom," said St. Augustine, and he was absolutely right. Patience needs the balance of wisdom – and it needs the balance of courage too.

Here are 5 reasons why the power of patience is so important in our life.

1. Patience helps us fulfill our dreams.

    If you are short of patience, even though your dream may be an admirable one, you will simply not have the strength and persistence necessary to sustain you through the inevitable disappointments and setbacks that life brings.

2. You need patience to become whole.

    What was true in ages past is still true today. As the Bible says (James 1.4), "Let patience have her perfect works, that ye may be perfect and entire, wanting nothing."

3. Patience is required to fully forgive.

    Sometimes, we may think we have forgiven someone for an injustice, but then pain and resentment rise up in us again. Do we give up and allow negative emotions to fester or do we summon the angel of patience to our aid and forgive at a deeper level?

4. Patience helps us see others in a clearer light.

    First impressions aren't always accurate, as we
    all know. It can take time and perseverance to
    see the true quality and worth of a person – to
    see their heart. "You don't see my heart," I
    would cry to JoAnn once in a while during the
    early days of our relationship. Well, perhaps
    she didn't. But I didn't see the depth of her
    loving, caring spirit for quite a while either. I'm
    sure glad we were both willing to let patience
    work its wondrous ways.

5. Patience nourishes other human virtues.

    As St. Augustine suggested, if we want to
    develop wisdom, we will need the help of its
    companion, patience. Cultivating compassion is
    essential too. Perhaps some people are born
    with naturally compassionate natures, but it's
    my guess that even compassion needs the
    nourishment of patience at times.

Chapter 38

The Art of Wellness

"The power of love to change bodies is legendary, built into folklore, common sense, and everyday experience. Love moves the flesh, it pushes matter around.... Throughout history, 'tender loving care' has uniformly been recognized as a valuable element in healing."
– Larry Dossey, M.D.

"Reading poetry gives me a sense of calm, well-being, and love for humanity – the same stuff more flexible women get from yoga."
– J. Courtney Sullivan

Do you sometimes feel discouraged or out of sorts but you're not quite sure what to do about it? Here's a solution that worked for me the other day.

Perhaps it was because I'd had a couple of minor procedures for skin cancer on my head and neck. Or perhaps it was because I was frustrated about my blog — uncertain about what direction I should take. In any case, I wasn't making much progress.

As I sat idly in my office pondering what my next step should be with the blog, an inner voice I know very well spoke up. "Why don't you vacuum the house?" it said. "You know it needs it."

I have to admit that my initial reaction to this idea was not favorable. After all, I had been successfully putting off this little chore (one of the contributions I make to the well-being of our home) for several days, if not weeks.

Life has taught me that sometimes when something seems counterintuitive, it's exactly what I need to do. I've also learned that when I give my best into some simple task, I feel good. And feel good I did, as I grabbed the vacuum and began venturing into every nook and cranny with all the energy and enthusiasm I could muster. It took me about 45 minutes to vacuum the house, after which it was time for lunch. Perfect.

Good food prepared with love is the foundation of wellness. My sweet wife had been thinking for some time about creating a new dish for lunch that would include two nutritious ingredients, black beans and kale, along with chicken.

So she took a can of black beans, and after washing and rinsing the beans, put them in the slow cooker along with chicken, kale, some onion and celery, and water. The result was wonderful. The slow cooker is one of my favorite inventions. It makes food so easy to swallow and digest, and so succulent.

The ingredients came together like a beautiful symphony, and by the time I was finished I fairly hummed with contentment. Wellness is not a destination. It's a lifestyle and a journey that calls for every bit of love and flexibility that is in us.

Chapter 39

Balance Is the Key to Well-Being

"A wise woman recognizes when her life is out of balance and summons the courage to act to correct it."
– Suze Orman

"A lot of people say they want to get out of pain, and I'm sure that's true, but they aren't willing to make healing a high priority. They aren't willing to look inside to see the source of their pain in order to deal with it."
– Lindsay Wagner

One day, while living in a beautiful part of British Columbia called the Cariboo, I suddenly developed a sore back. There was no reason for it that I was aware of, but it was so painful that I went to see a doctor. I can still remember his face as he checked me over and finally said, "We like to be conservative in a situation like this. I want you to lie down and rest for three or four days."

I didn't know any better, and proceeded to do just what the doctor ordered. Unfortunately, I didn't get better, I got worse. My back became more and more sore and I developed sciatica in my right leg. It got to the point where I could hardly bear to touch my foot to the floor.

What followed was a month of pure misery as I basically withdrew from life. Not a smart move at all. I got discouraged and depressed. I began to lose weight and spent a lot of time at home feeling sorry for myself.

Finally, one spring afternoon, I rebelled at my sad plight and decided to go for a walk in the meadow at the back of our house.

As I was walking slowly and painfully along a forest path, I stopped for some reason and looked at a small tree growing beside the path. "This tree is whole and well," I thought to myself, "why can't I be whole and well too?"

My whole unhappy situation changed in that very moment. It was as if the tree was a catalyst that shook me out of my sorry state. I got hold of a book of back exercises and began doing the exercises with fervor and dedication. I fell in love with them, and within a week I was well on the way to recovery.

I agree absolutely with some research from Wayne State University in Michigan that I came across recently. The report from the Counseling and Psychological Services of WSU described how wellness is an overall balance of social, intellectual, spiritual, emotional, physical and occupational wellness.

The report summed up this kind of balanced approach to wellness as follows:

1. A direction which by its nature, moves us toward a more proactive, responsible and healthier existence.

2. The integration of the body, mind and spirit.

3. The loving acceptance of ourselves today and exciting free search for who we choose to become tomorrow.

4. Living by choice; a completion of the daily decisions we make that lead us to that person we choose to become.

I love these wise words. If I learned anything during my sad ordeal those many years ago it is that life loves balance – and will lead us toward healing and wholeness as we trust our own instincts and seek balance in our lives.

Chapter 40

Learning to Breathe Like a Baby Again

"Breath is the bridge which connects life to consciousness, which unites your body to your thoughts. Whenever your mind becomes scattered, use your breath as the means to take hold of your mind again."

– Thich Nhat Hanh

"Practicing regular, mindful breathing can be calming and energizing and can even help with stress-related health problems ranging from panic attacks to digestive disorders."

– Andrew Weil, M.D.

I find that taking a few minutes now and again, especially in the evening, to deliberately breathe with my belly does wonders for my health and well-being. I feel renewed. I relax, enfolded in peace from head to toe.

When we were babies, we breathed naturally through our abdomen. Nice, relaxed, natural breathing the way Nature intended. Unfortunately, as we grow up and succumb to the pressures and anxieties of modern life, we tend to forget all about natural breathing and begin to breathe through our chest.

It doesn't work nearly as well. It is not nearly as relaxed or peaceful a process. Our breathing becomes shallow, and we lose the calming, soothing effect of abdominal breathing. In some ways our breathing becomes a struggle that mirrors a larger struggle as we try to stay sane and find happiness in a violent, unpredictable world.

A recent study in Sweden discovered that 83% of adults breathe through their chest. Of course, this has various side effects. For instance, we have to take more breaths per minute, while at the same time we receive less oxygen and expel fewer waste products.

I have found that even a small amount of effort and time devoted to relearning how to breathe like a child brings great rewards, especially as we age. It helps improve my blood pressure, for example. If I'm facing a situation that I know will make me anxious, breathing with my belly helps me stay calm.

You can find all kinds of advice about proper breathing on the Internet and elsewhere, of course. I am not an expert, obviously, but I thought I'd share my own experience in this area – what works for me – in case it is useful to you. So here goes.

First, I sit down in my favorite chair. Some suggest lying down when you begin to learn abdominal breathing, which is good advice, I'm sure.

I seem to remember reading once that to improve our breathing it's good to squeeze all the old breath out of our belly first, whereupon our belly will naturally fill with new air. There may be value to this approach but personally, I don't like the effort that it entails. I find that if I keep my chest perfectly still like a sleeping alligator, the rest more or less takes care of itself. I mean, if you want to stay alive and you can't breathe with your chest, how else can you breathe except by pushing your belly in and out like a pair of bellows?

So this is what works for me. I like to do two sets of abdominal breathing each evening, seated, as I say, in my favorite chair. It's never too late to learn to breathe like child again.

Chapter 41

6 Steps to Contentment

"At some point, you gotta let go, and sit still, and allow contentment to come to you."
>   – Elizabeth Gilbert

"Whatever we are waiting for – peace of mind, contentment, grace, the inner awareness of simple abundance – it will surely come to us, but only when we are ready to receive it with an open and grateful heart."
>   – Sarah Ban Breathnach

When I was 12 or 13 – knowing how much I loved boats and the water – my parents took me on a holiday to a beautiful region of England called the Norfolk Broads. We lived for a week on a houseboat on the River Bure near Horning and I thought I had gone to heaven.

A small rowing boat was provided for our use and the first thing Dad said to me when we arrived was: "You can be in charge of the dinghy." I was ecstatic. Each morning, as soon as I woke up—

long before my parents opened their eyes—I climbed into the boat and disappeared to explore the river.

The author sails his first boat on the Blackwater River.

I had an exciting book by an author named Stanley Weyman which I took with me to a quiet, secluded spot. If there is such a thing as contentment, this was it. Sitting in my little boat, with my nose in my book, surrounded by water, trees, birds, and peace. Only when I got hungry did I put my book away and row back to the houseboat.

Here are six steps that I find helpful in creating calm and contentment in life.

1. Be willing to forgive.

    How can we be content if we carry the pain of past injustice with us wherever we go? The quicker we can let go of old wounds or insults and forgive whoever needs forgiving in our life, the sooner we will experience the happiness that is our true destiny. Our minds are designed to be supple and flexible. The mind answers to us, we don't answer to it.

2.   Don't be hostage to your goals.

We need goals in life, of course. We need dreams, and we need to follow our dreams. But there is a curious paradox here – a kind of creative tension – because we should not be held hostage to our dreams. For example, this book is important to me. It's my "baby." I enjoy writing it, and I want it to succeed, and bless the world. But something else is more important: being true to myself.

3.   Don't take your thoughts too seriously.

Some people become troubled when unruly or unpleasant thoughts arise in their mind. They wish the thoughts would go away. But really, what do those errant thoughts matter? Do they have any real power? No. They don't. Let them do whatever they want to do and thank God for the timeless contentment that already exists in the sanctity of your own being.

As Socrates wisely declared: "Contentment is natural wealth, luxury is artificial poverty."

4.   Give your gift.

What is the unique gift you bring to this world? Think about this. See if you can describe your gift in a single sentence. We are not just talking about a particular role or activity here, though that's included, but the unique spirit, or essence that is yours. Knowing what our gift is and giving it freely, consistently and with love is a sure path to contentment.

5. Listen to your inner wisdom.

   Contentment and wisdom go arm in arm. Even as I write these words a mental image comes to my mind of a pair of young lovers strolling blissfully together in a sunlit garden. If you would know more contentment in your life, be still, and listen to the quiet voice of wisdom speaking to you right now from the depths of your soul.

6. Take a moment to be still.

   Stillness is the very source of contentment. It is the womb where contentment is born. Make stillness your friend. Make a habit of appreciating stillness. In stillness troubles fade away. And in stillness we find the wisdom we need to meet life's challenges and fulfill our dreams.

   God be with you. My wish for you is my wish for myself, to see every challenge as a gift that can help us grow and become more alive, more whole and more content.

What's Your Next Step?

If you enjoyed this book and would like to share in nurturing a more positive approach to aging, here are some possibilities:

- Email friends and acquaintances to let them know about this book, perhaps sharing some of your own thoughts on this topic.
- Write a letter to your local newspaper about aging or invite some friends in to discuss this important subject.
- Submit a review of my book to Amazon. This would be a huge help. It really would.
- Email me at christopherfoster@comcast.net and share your own experiences, feedback or ideas with me. Again, I would be most grateful.

Please remember that as you do pass the word along about this book to others, or share some of your thoughts on aging with them, you may find that you have touched someone's life in a most remarkable way.

Afterword

The True Promise of Aging

By Carol Leavenworth, Jungian psychotherapist

In his final years of driving, my father Frank would climb into his big white Buick for a trip into town, insert the key into the ignition and pause before backing out of the garage.

"Where am I?" he would muse.

Then, "Where am I going?"

And finally he would ask himself, "How do I get there?"

Dad wasn't one to give advice or pass along life lessons. But here, I thought, was some important wisdom. These are questions we could all be asking ourselves and not just when we're in the car.

I learned a lot from Dad down the years. He taught me highway driving and how to balance a checkbook along with many other things. But his most important lessons – like this one – were imparted indirectly.

Sometimes toward the end of his days, I would ask him to tell me about the essential things that his long life taught him. He would become shy and change the subject.

Maybe he was afraid that if he opened up, he would be misunderstood or dismissed. Probably this had happened to him before. If it had, he would not have been alone.

Young and old, we are all victims of a pervasive and insidious cultural ageism. Our elders are trivialized and often ignored. We look at the elderly and see bodies that are in decline. We see white hair and wrinkled skin. And we want to turn away.

We tend to think of the old as failing adults with nothing much to say that is relevant to busy adult lives. We haven't been taught that there is another stage of psychological development waiting for us all beyond adulthood. We seldom hear about the happiness that characterizes this final period of life. We don't understand that our elders know the answers to questions we have been asking ourselves since adolescence.

This is why I was excited when Christopher Foster offered to share his latest work, *The Secret Promise of Aging: Finding Meaning, Joy and Inner Peace as Years Fly By*. Chris is in the vanguard of a growing number of elders committed to letting the rest of us in on important realizations to be found on the other side of the great demarcation between adulthood and elder hood.

The Secret Promise of Aging goes to the heart of the mystery surrounding life's final developmental stage. In his first chapter, Chris reveals key secrets to the joy and peace of mind that led him to the bliss he is discovering in his later years.

Chris goes on to tell us exactly what his personal experience has taught him about the love within each one of us and the happiness that is hiding everywhere in plain sight. And he doesn't stop there. He shares specific details about his personal path to profound inner wisdom – the wisdom he believes any of us may discover deep within.

Acknowledging that each individual's journey is unique, Chris encourages us to seek out our own happiness and bliss. With the confidence that arises out of authentic personal experience, he points the way to self-realization. And he shows us exactly how to explore this path for ourselves.

When I asked my ninety-year-old father to tell me his secret to long life, he answered, "Don't die."

I would add this to Dad's advice: "Don't die before you read Chris Foster's amazing little book, *The Secret Promise of Aging*."

Carol Leavenworth is a psychotherapist in Denver, Colorado.

About Christopher Foster

I was born in London in 1932. An only child, I lived a normal British middle class life (if you don't count WWII) until I was 16, when I told my parents at lunch one day that I wanted to find the truth of life. It didn't go over well. Dad and I got into a fierce argument which ended suddenly when he lost his temper and slapped me hard across the face.

Dad was a wonderful man of great integrity but he never was able to heal the rages that overtook him from time to time. He was a reporter, and I followed in his footsteps, working on newspapers and magazines in London, Southern Rhodesia (now Zimbabwe), and New Zealand. When I was 23, my longing to find deeper meaning in life took me to British Columbia. I worked briefly on a ranch and then got a job as a reporter on the *Daily Colonist* in Victoria, BC.

Life works in mysterious ways sometimes, for sure. Through a remarkable synchronicity I met a British nobleman in Vancouver who became my mentor and changed my life. His name was Lord Martin Cecil and he was a descendant of Lord Burghley, chief adviser to Queen Elizabeth I.

As a young man, Lord Martin had himself rebelled against the traditions of the British aristocracy, giving up the comfortable life that awaited him at Burghley House – the stately English mansion where he had been born – to manage his father's cattle ranch in a remote area of British Columbia. It was a hard life made even harder by the burden of the Great Depression.

I was drawn to Martin the moment I met him. I became part of a community he had founded in BC with a simple purpose: To express in practical ways in our living the same steadfast, beautiful character revealed by Jesus and other great prophets.

Was it an ambitious purpose? Perhaps it was. But it was a magnet to me and quite a number of other people of various ages, cultures and backgrounds who were drawn to participate in such a remarkable adventure.

The community was a cooperative venture and we worked at various tasks to help support it. For example, my first job was stocking shelves in a nearby supermarket. For many years I edited the local weekly newspaper. Then my late wife, Joy, and I founded a newsletter named *Integrity* and made nine trips to India and other countries to promote ideals such as integrity and universal spiritual values. The community gradually dissolved after Lord Martin died and following Joy's death in 1991 I moved to the U.S.

I've loved writing all my life. I wrote my first story in an old scrapbook at the age of 8 while living with my mother in an apartment block in London during the early days of the Blitz. I was later evacuated and sent to live with my aunt in the Devon countryside. My brave, indomitable father served as a war correspondent in India and the Far East. He sometimes accompanied British and Allied troops in landings against the Japanese – armed with a typewriter instead of a gun.

I have written five books, including a biography of Lord Martin Cecil entitled *One Heart, One Way*, which is the Burghley family motto. My last book was a fable entitled *The Raven Who Spoke with God*, which I wrote in a Denver coffee shop soon after moving to Colorado to marry JoAnn. The book was published on 9/11 and has been published in 10 foreign language editions.

I began blogging in 2009. I'd be thrilled if you'd like to take a look at my blog and share your experiences or thoughts about aging.

Visit me at www.thehappyseeker.com.

An Inspiring Story about a Choice We All Must Face

Christopher Foster's *The Raven Who Spoke with God*, translated into ten languages, is an inspiring story about a choice we all have to make in life. Will we listen to the sometimes fearful or discouraging voices around us – or will we listen to our own inner voice?

Joshua is a brave young raven torn between following his dream to restore the honor of the raven or settling for the humdrum existence of his parents and siblings.

Alone, scared and hungry, Joshua risks everything as he leaves his home and embarks on a journey into the unknown. Along the way he learns three crucial lessons vital to us all:

There is an unquenchable source of courage within each one of us that will bring us safely through any challenge we may face.

As we listen to the nudges of our own heart the next step always emerges.

As we are true to ourselves, we will discover new friends and mentors who help us on our journey.

Praise for
The Raven Who Spoke with God

"It soars. This is no ordinary book, and no ordinary bird."
> – *Sunday Oklahoman*

"A wonderful tale, very well written and filled with love and wisdom. Now that I've read The Raven, *I will loan my copy to a friend who loves animals and is having a hard time finding direction and purpose."*
> – Robert Gerzon, author,
> *Finding Serenity in The Age of Anxiety*

"A fun book that can be enjoyed by readers of all ages."
> – *Clarion-Ledger*, Jackson, Mississippi

"It reminded me of a Jonathan Livingston Seagull *in the Rockies."*
> – Bob Spear, *Heartland Reviews*

"A magical fable that illuminates many truths yet never preaches. Gentle, touching, and a perfect vehicle for deep conversation."
> – *Communaissance* magazine

"The writing is lyrical and the story is inspirational and uplifting."
> – *Green Bay Press-Gazette*

"A sweet fable about living in the joy of the present, featuring a young raven named Joshua who learns to

look to his heart, to the stillness within, for answers to every despair." — *The Boox Review*

For more information about *The Raven Who Spoke with God*, available at Amazon as a Kindle e-book, please visit:
http://www.amazon.com/dp/B007OLLQYM

41049635R00127

Made in the USA
Lexington, KY
27 April 2015